ABOUT THIS BOOK

The whole world in one city – not merely a trite advertising slogan but a reality: in the truest sense of the word, London is a metropolis, formed by people arriving from every corner of the earth, bringing their culture with them to create the special – although not always harmonious – mixture that lies at the heart of the British capital. This variety is not based only on the interplay of cultural peculiarities, however, but also on the innovations of a society whose technical inventions and artistic creativity have made an essential contribution to the economy of Europe. Summing up London is no simple matter. It is not just the sheer size, although this is indeed overwhelming – it is that there is so much to do and so many sights to see. Regal London has its imposing palaces, commercial London its ground-breaking architecture and first-class

shopping – while historic London has its cathedrals and the City (the original settlement, now the capital's financial hub), not to mention maritime London at Greenwich and, of course, the city's main artery, the River Thames. There's also the London of art and culture, with some of the most notable collections in the world distributed among countless museums and galleries, and the stage with performances of every playwright from Shakespeare and Sheridan to Bennett and Beckett, along with all forms of musical entertainment. This illustrated book is intended to give a modest cross-section of this wonderful city, from its historic buildings, through its parks, both formal and informal, to the everyday residential areas. Beyond the world-famous sights, London still has surprises even for those who have spent all their lives here.

In the heart of the West End, the magnificent façade of the National Gallery proudly overlooks Trafalgar Square. With Nelson keeping a watchful eye on proceedings from his lofty platform, the square is a popular meeting point for tourists and also the scene of numerous events and festivals throughout the year. Thousands of people gather on the square every year to see in the New Year.

CONTENTS

CONTENTS

THE CITY OF LONDON

The City of London – the City, for short – is the historic heart of the capital. It has its roots in the Roman town of Londinium, and its size – one square mile (just over 2.5 square kilometres) – has not changed since the Middle Ages. Alongside New York, London is the world's leading financial capital, and by day the City is a thriving hub of international business. But at night, when the people who work in its glass palaces go home, the City is like a ghost town. When Londoners talk of 'the City', they often refer to London's financial industry, though many finance companies are now located in Docklands.

Modernity and tradition combine in a surprisingly harmonious way in the City of London: the imposing dome of St Paul's Cathedral seems quite at home amid the new temples of finance – history and faith in the future are the twin supports of the City.

THE TOWER OF LONDON

The massive riverside fortress watching over the capital from its position on the eastern edge of the City bears the formidable title Her Majesty's Royal Palace and Fortress The Tower of London – better known simply as the Tower. At its heart stands the White Tower, a mighty fortification built by William the Conqueror in 1078, soon after he was crowned king of England. It was intended to protect London from attack, while at the same time providing the Norman rulers with a perfect viewpoint from which to keep an ever-vigilant eye on the self-assured inhabitants of the independent city. The Tower's two walls and its moat were added in the 12th and 13th centuries. The complex continued to serve as a royal residence until the 17th century, and was still being used as a prison in the 20th century. Today it houses the Jewel House, where the British crown jewels have been on display for over 300 years.

The fortress on the river (left and below left) receives countless visitors each year, not just because of its history of rolling heads and squabbling nobility imprisoned in its dungeons, but also because of its traditional pageantry. The yeoman warders, also known as Beefeaters (below right), who notionally guard the Tower (now bereft of prisoners) and the Crown Jewels, have now become a tourist attraction.

TOWER BRIDGE

Opened in 1894, Tower Bridge is not only one of London's leading landmarks, but also a great testimony to the ingenious Victorian engineers who built it. By the middle of the 19th century, London's East End had become so densely populated that a new river crossing was essential. The new bridge would, however, be the first to be constructed east of London Bridge, an area previously declared off-limits for fear of impeding the ships using the docks in the east of the city. The answer was to combine a bascule bridge with a suspension bridge. Steam engines were used to power a hydraulic system capable of opening the bridge within a matter of minutes. Today, the bridge is powered by electricity, and the two towers house an exhibition that describes its history. The upper walkway has now been glazed in, and offers a commanding view over the city and its river.

ALL HALLOWS BY THE TOWER / THE MONUMENT

The Monument commemorates the greatest catastrophe in London's history, the Great Fire, which almost completely destroyed the densely inhabited medieval city in 1666. Christopher Wren, London's great architect, designed the column, which was finally erected in 1677 and stands about 60 metres (200 feet) from the bakery in Pudding Lane where the fire broke out. In those days, the City of London was mainly composed of wooden houses with thatched roofs. The fire also destroyed the old St Paul's Cathedral and more than 80 parish churches. One of the churches spared by the fire was All Hallows by the Tower; many more were rebuilt by Wren. There is a fine view over the city from the top of the Monument, 60 metres (200 feet) above street level, revealing a panorama of buildings, now in stone, proof of the City's will to survive.

Beautiful by day or by night: Tower Bridge looks like a monument symbolizing the connection between historic and modern London. A few technical details: the towers are 65 metres (214 feet) high, the road surface is 9 metres (30 feet) above the water and the pedestrian bridge 34 metres (113) feet above that. The central section is raised several times a day to allow larger boats to pass.

All Hallows by the Tower (left) is the oldest church in the city and is older even than the Tower of London. Its origins date back to 675. Rebuilt several times in the ensuing centuries, the oldest sections are the remains of a building from the Roman period, parts of which are exhibited in the undercroft museum in the crypt. Below: The Monument to the Great Fire of London on Fish Street.

LLOYD'S OF LONDON

At night, the gleaming steel and glass façade of the dramatically lit Lloyd's Building is imbued with an almost otherworldly glow. By day, the external glass elevators, stairwells and service pipes make the building look as if it has been turned inside out – which is exactly the impression that its architect, Richard Rogers, set out to create. When the building was opened in 1986, Roger's innovative, award-winning design was hailed as an architectural sensation, paving the way for the more ambitious building projects that London has witnessed since. For Lloyd's of London, Roger's steel palace was a long way from the insurance market's first home inside Edward Lloyd's coffee house in 1688. As the centuries rolled on, Lloyd's grew to become a giant of the insurance industry, catering for the most complicated of risks – even arranging to insure the legs of the world's most beautiful supermodels.

The Lloyd's Building, comprising several office blocks and auxiliary towers arranged around a rectangular square, is a complex with an almost futuristic air. Its features include the stainless-steel spiral stairwells that wind round the outside walls and the 12 glass exterior elevators, which were the first of their kind in Britain. The large Underwriting Room houses the famous Lutine Bell.

LEADENHALL MARKET

There has been a market on this site since the Middle Ages, allowing the local rural population to sell its produce, mainly poultry, meat and fish. The first stalls were grouped round a town house with a lead roof, which gave the market its name, but a stone hall was not constructed here until after the Great Fire of London in the 17th century. The new covered structure was divided into the Beef Market, the Green Yard and the Herb Market. Today's magnificent building, an elaborate Victorian structure of wrought-iron and glass, was designed by Sir Horace Jones and dates back to 1881. The shop and restaurant façades lining the cobbled passageways have been retained in the same style. The market, which is very photogenic, is not only a tourist attraction – it was also used as the set for Diagon Alley in the 2001 film 'Harry Potter and the Philospher's Stone'.

The shops in the market sell fine delicatessen, meat, cheese, fish and other provisions, as well as smart leather goods, designer suits, stationery and pens, and other high value items for well-off business types who work in the area. There are plenty of restaurants and pubs offering refreshments and – if you have sufficient funds at your disposal – you can hire the hall for private functions.

THE BANK OF ENGLAND / THE ROYAL EXCHANGE

The Royal Exchange was founded in 1565. The present neoclassical building, which opened in 1844, is its third premises. The future Bank of England was founded in 1694, when the Scottish financier William Paterson offered the cash-strapped government of King James II a loan of £1.2 million. The Bank of England was established and was soon doing a roaring trade. Its first home on Walbrook stood on the site of the Roman Temple of Mithras, although the latter's foundations were only discovered in 1954. In 1734, the bank moved to Threadneedle Street. Designed by Sir John Soane in the neoclassical style, much of the interior was demolished in the 1920s to make way for Sir Herbert Baker's redesign, which, branded an act of vandalism by some critics, was not universally welcomed. You'll find the extensive Bank of England Museum on the eastern side of the building.

Breakfast at Tiffany's: opposite the Bank of England (below), the Royal Exchange is a monument to wealth. Vast sums of money are no longer traded on the magnificent hall floor of the former stock exchange. Instead, expensive, opulent goods from luxury brand names such as Gucci, Cartier, Hermès and Tiffany tempt the rich and beautiful in very smart surroundings.

THE GUILDHALL

The Guildhall has been the seat of government in the City of London since the Middle Ages, and the medieval building remains the representative home of the City authorities today. The building's walls, at least, date from the early 15th century, making the Guildhall one of the oldest buildings in London. The splendid Great Hall is used for civic functions, held beneath the coats of arms of the 12 guilds whose representatives once ran the City with unimpeded power. The glorious medieval crypts with their vaulted ceilings are located beneath the Great Hall. The clock museum is just one of the many attractions in the western part of the Guildhall, and the art gallery is housed in another section of the building. Pictures dating from various periods of the city's history are on display here, and a visit to the gallery is also an opportunity to see the remains of a Roman arena.

The Guildhall is one of the most venerable buildings in the City. Nowadays it is principally used for state occasions, but it also houses an art gallery (left and below left). Below right: The figures of Gog and Magog, two mythical giants who, according to legend, were captured and chained up here to guard the gates of the Guildhall. Wicker models of the figures are displayed at the annual Lord Mayor's Show.

THE CITY OF LONDON

The glittering power of money: the City of London is the world's leading financial centre and an important contributor to the British economy. More than 13,000 companies are based in the Square Mile, including 500 banks and all the world's leading finance houses. All the British financial institutions have their headquarters here, including the London Stock Exchange, the giant insurance company Lloyd's of London and the Bank of England. Billions are traded every day, and even the credit crunch has failed to change things very much – capitalism here is still far from dead. In the evening and at weekends, however, the area is quite deserted and even the pubs and restaurants often close their doors. Only about 8,000 people actually live here, mostly on the Barbican estate, a complex of concrete blocks built in the 1960s.

PUBS

The traditional pub lies at the very heart of the British psyche, an institution that has been the focus of social life for as long as anyone can remember. Its origins can be traced back to Roman Britain, when places of refreshment grew up at strategic intervals along the network of roads built by the colonizing Romans. As well as a welcome stop for those on the road, these inns soon became places where people could meet up to gossip or discuss local matters. The earliest version of the pub sign was a small evergreen bush hung outside an inn, while the pub sign as it is known today began to develop in the Middle Ages. Ale remained the tipple of choice for the masses until gin palaces became popular in the early 18th century. In 1869, the Wine and Beerhouse Act restricted the hours during which alcohol could be sold and in 1914 'last orders' were set at 11 pm, a time that remained in force until 2005. There are several contenders for the position of London's oldest pub, among which are: the Prospect of Whitby in Wapping, popular with smugglers and reputedly a haunt of Dickens, Pepys and Whistler; the George Inn, Borough High Street; the Lamb & Flag, Covent Garden; and the Cittie of York, Holborn, on the site of a 1420 tavern, though the present building has a later date.

Britain's first skyscraper was built in the City – Tower 42, which at 183 metres (600 feet) and 42 levels is still the tallest building in the City of London, followed closely by 30 St Mary Axe, also known as the Swiss Re Building, whose characteristic shape has earned it the name 'the Gherkin'. Further skyscrapers are planned or under construction, and the 'Pinnacle' office tower is planned to be London's tallest building.

The classic pint of ale, a little more than half a litre (left), or a leisurely gin and tonic after work or shopping is often enjoyed standing at the bar and is a fixed point in the day for London's magical Victorian pubs. Many pubs, such as the Sherlock Holmes (below left), contain rich wood-panelling and brass fittings. and are lovingly decorated with souvenirs and mementos.

THE BARBICAN

This massive complex rose up from a derelict patch of land on the edge of the City in the 1960s and 1970s. Designed by modernist architectural firm Chamberlin, Powell and Bon, its Brutalist style was born of a desire to build on a gargantuan scale. The first buildings erected were high-rise apartments. These concrete giants were typical of their time, and could have easily become the hotspots of social breakdown with which similar buildings became synonymous. The Barbican, however, had a narrow escape, thanks in large part to its arts complex. The biggest venue of its kind in Europe, it won over Londoners with its impressive calendar of events. Both the London Symphony Orchestra and the BBC Symphony Orchestra made the Barbican their home, and audiences still flock here to enjoy drama, cinema and ballet. The Barbican Gallery, meanwhile, hosts excellent photographic exhibitions.

The star of the complex is the Barbican Centre, Europe's largest cultural centre, a popular venue among Londoners for the quality of the performances held there. Concerts, drama, film and ballet, as well as the likes of the Merce Cunningham Dance Company and the theatre project 'The Elephant Vanishes', have met with enthusiastic receptions, as have the Barbican Gallery's photographic exhibitions.

Seddon House

ST PAUL'S CATHEDRAL

Standing proudly over the palatial offices of the City's financial institutions, the splendid façade and dome of St Paul's Cathedral are hard to ignore. There has been a Christian church located here on Ludgate Hill for some 1,400 years. Built in the English baroque style, the current cathedral is St Paul's fifth and without question most impressive incarnation. Its medieval predecessor was a casualty of the Great Fire of 1666, which destroyed almost the entire city. Sir Christopher Wren was the architect charged with rebuilding both St Paul's and some 50 other devastated London churches. His designs were repeatedly rejected before the first stone of the new building was finally laid in 1677. The first service in the new St Paul's Cathedral took place 20 years after that, and Christopher Wren would later become the first of many great Britons to be buried there.

Based on St Peter's in Rome, the elegant dome (left) of London's most beautiful church has become a symbol and hallmark of the city. Its unique baroque magnificence, with airy verticals, highly decorated figures and rich ornamentation, is if anything atypical of the rather sober England of the time, and was indeed considered too 'Papist' by some contemporaries.

THE OLD BAILEY

A good TV murder mystery can be enough to keep you awake at night, and the best courtroom dramas can keep you on the edge of your seat, but neither is a patch on a real trial at London's Central Criminal Court. This architecturally uninspiring building is the venue for some of the world's most spectacular court cases, making headlines in Britain and beyond. In a previous building, the controversial writer Oscar Wilde stood trial at the Old Bailey, and it was here, in 1990, that the Guildford Four had their convictions as IRA terrorists quashed – finally proving their innocence after 15 years in prison. The Yorkshire Ripper, by contrast, was sentenced to life imprisonment at the Old Bailey in 1981. The site of the building itself has a grim, and well-known, past – until 1902, this was the location of Newgate Prison, where convicts sentenced to death were sometimes publicly executed.

Judgment has been passed for centuries in the world's most famous courthouse and the public has always been allowed to be present. The death penalty was often handed down in the past and execution by hanging was still a possibility into the 20th century, most often for murder. Capital punishment for picking pockets was abolished in 1808, but it was not abolished for murder until 1969.

ST BRIDE'S

The elegant steeple of St Bride's Church is a familiar feature of the London skyline. Built in the baroque style, it is, after St Paul's, the tallest of the churches designed by Sir Christopher Wren. Originally consecrated to the Irish saint Bridgit of Kildare, St Bride's may also be London's oldest church. It is located on Fleet Street – the traditional home of London's newspaper and printing industries – and became the church of choice of London's publishers and journalists. There is an exhibition about London's printing industry located in the crypt, and although the British press has largely moved to the Docklands area, its members still come to St Bride's for quiet reflection. Inside the church, a selection of posters, cards, candles and photographs pay tribute to the fearless journalists of all religions and backgrounds who have given their lives in the service of their profession.

Arranged in several tiers and elaborately decorated, tapering to a point, the spire of St Bride's could easily be likened to a classic wedding cake. The interior is less opulent than Wren's masterpiece, St Paul's Cathedral, and already shows signs of a more elegant classicism. The church was destroyed by German bombs in World War II and has been lovingly restored.

THE CITY OF WESTMINSTER

Westminster is generally associated with the British government, but the district includes a lot more than just the seat of power at Whitehall; encompassing the West End, it is also the major cultural focus of London. Since the 17th century, the rich and powerful have preferred to live here, west of the City, where the air was cleaner and there was enough space to build large mansions, cultivate lofty pleasures and purchase fine goods. Westminster is thus the location of many of London's most famous sights, most of its theatres and museums, and the best shopping areas.

Tradition and modernity: the London Eye and the Palace of Westminster. Until the 16th century, the seat of the House of Lords and the Commons was a private residence, and was used for parliamentary purposes only later. The current building was erected in the 19th century.

THE STRAND

The Strand has been the connecting road between the Palace of Westminster and the City of London since the Middle Ages. It was once lined with the magnificent palaces of nobles and bishops, but of these only Somerset House has survived. All that remains of the Savoy Palace, a splendid medieval residence, is the name. The palace was destroyed in the Peasant's Revolt of 1381 and the Savoy Hotel now stands on its site. The Strand and its theatres were a cultural centre in the Victorian era, but nowadays it is a less spectacular arterial road connecting Trafalgar Square and Fleet Street. The crossing point between these two streets, Temple Bar, was once the westernmost extent of the City and is commemorated with an 1880 monument of a gryphon, a winged lion with an eagle's head, which guards the gates to the city by the Royal Courts of Justice.

The main entrance to the Royal Courts of Justice (far left) is in the Strand, but this neo-Gothic building with its 140-metre (470-foot) façade is almost a town by itself. It is the seat of the Court of Appeals and the High Court of Justice and is surrounded by the Inns of Court, the four barristers' associations. The City limits are marked by the Temple Bar Memorial (below). A street preacher entertains passers-by (left).

SOMERSET HOUSE

Somerset House once provided offices for the tax authorities, and its transformation into a centre of art, culture and entertainment was a sheer stroke of genius. The neoclassical structure was erected at the end of the 18th century to house a number of academic and royal societies, and in this sense it was the first public service building. But it was the arrival of numerous cultural institutions that secured the building's place in the affections of Londoners. Today it is home to the Courtauld Institute of Art with its collection of old masters and Impressionist paintings, as well as the new Embankment Galleries (see opposite); it is also the London base of St Petersburg's magnificent State Hermitage Museum. The inner courtyard is the ultimate jewel in the crown: in summer, 55 fountains fill the space, making way for London's most beautiful and romantic ice rink in winter.

Pure culture: Somerset House is not just where you will find classic art (left, the Courtauld Gallery collection) but is also an all-year-round entertainment centre, with an open-air cinema, rock concerts in the summer and an ice rink at Christmas. There are also art exhibitions, readings by respected literary figures, adult education events and a terrace restaurant with a cocktail bar.

COVENT GARDEN / ROYAL OPERA HOUSE

Covent Garden has been a focus of popular entertainment since the 17th century. It all started with the market, formerly a fruit and vegetable market, which still attracts countless sightseers and shoppers today, and it wasn't long before all sorts of street entertainers and itinerant artists were also drawn to Covent Garden. In the 18th century, John Gay's 'Beggar's Opera', which distinguished itself from court opera by targeting a popular audience, proved so successful that it soon required a stage of its own. Thus was born the Theatre Royal, a venue that became synonymous with great, popular art. The Theatre Royal's building later became the Royal Opera, one of the world's foremost opera houses. The area around Covent Garden, meanwhile, continues to be a hub of entertainment. True to its history, there is something for everyone – with popular culture at the top of the agenda.

The old Covent Garden Market, nowadays known as Covent Garden Piazza, is a glass-roofed building with an overwhelming array of boutiques and cafés and street artists, who entertain passers-by on the square outside. The famed Royal Opera House stages not only opera (left, a scene from Puccini's 'Turandot') but also ballet and drama, featuring international artists.

TRAFALGAR SQUARE

You can almost read the entire history of the British empire from Trafalgar Square, which also reflects the many faces of contemporary Britain. Situated at the heart of the West End, Trafalgar Square is named after one of the most significant battles fought by the British against Napoleon. It was at Trafalgar, off south-west Spain, that the British navy defeated the Spanish and French armada. Legendary naval hero Lord Nelson died in the battle, and the column erected in his memory dominates the square. The bronze lions at the base of the column are said to have been cast from canons captured from the French. Yet despite this backdrop of past glory and heroic achievement, Trafalgar Square has been the scene of the biggest demonstrations and parties ever witnessed in the capital, including the traditional New Year's celebrations – when thousands of Londoners gather to ring in the new year.

The classical façade of the National Gallery forms an elegant backdrop to the square (below), while its centre is marked by the 52-metre (170-foot) tall Nelson's Column with its four guardian lion statues – a Mecca for tourists. The fountain that stands in front of the 18th-century St Martin-in-the-Fields church dates back to the 1930s. Designed by Sir Edwin Lutyens, it is now a listed structure.

THE NATIONAL GALLERY / THE NATIONAL PORTRAIT GALLERY

In 1824, the British government purchased 38 pictures from the collection of the deceased banker John Julius Angerstein. The pictures were initially displayed in Angerstein's Pall Mall townhouse, moving to a new home on Trafalgar Square when the present National Gallery building was completed in 1838. Envisaged as a venue open to all social classes, today some 2,300 paintings from all the European schools and all historical periods are on permanent display in its galleries, among them some of the most important works by such masters as van Gogh, Monet, Leonardo da Vinci, Cézanne and Titian. The National Portrait Gallery is situated just around the corner on St Martin's Place. Its focus is not on the artists but on their subjects, and the gallery is a visual 'Who's Who' of the great and good of British history and culture, as depicted in paintings, sculptures and photographs.

The National Gallery houses an impressive collection of paintings – below right: 'A Woman' by Robert Campin, c. 1435. The National Portrait Gallery has numerous portraits of characters from British history, including oil paintings, photographs, drawings, sculptures and even caricatures. Pictures of kings and queens are very popular, offering a pictorial history of British royalty.

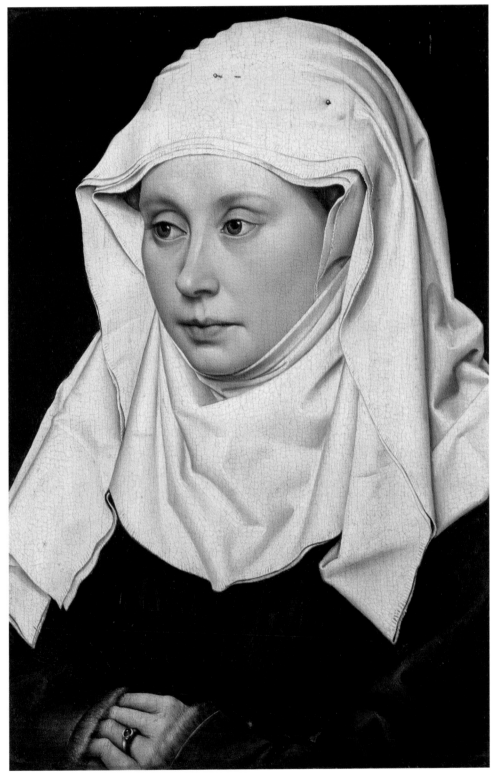

LEICESTER SQUARE

Robert Sidney, the second Earl of Leicester, who built a small palace here in the 17th century and was determined to keep the locals off his land, must be turning in his grave. Nowadays Leicester Square is the pedestrianized hub of London's nightlife and is always brimming with crowds of people, especially during the evening and early hours of the night. Buskers and street entertainers rub shoulders with tourists and Londoners out for a night on the town. Big film premieres are held here and the European success of blockbusters is decided as the stars parade on the red carpet. An array of nightclubs, bars, cafés, pubs and restaurants line the square and its immediate vicinity. In the middle of the square itself is a small fenced garden displaying several busts and statues, with that of Charlie Chaplin being the most recent addition.

Leicester Square's greatest attraction is people-watching, best carried out from one of the many street cafés. Who knows if a film star might suddenly make an appearance? The handprints of a number of stars are mounted in plaques set into the pavement. You can even enjoy your own 15 minutes of fame here, even if it is only from one of the caricaturists or portrait artists (left).

SOHO

The lively area of Soho has welcomed newcomers almost since its very beginnings, from the Protestant Huguenots who fled persecution in France and settled here in the late 16th century to the Chinese immigrants who turned the area around Gerrard Street into their own little piece of China after World War II (see page 66). More than anything, however, Soho was a place where bohemian culture flourished. Aspiring artists, writers and musicians all found refuge here, and if it wasn't for the distractions of the area's plentiful supply of bars and pubs, their talents might well have created a more enduring legacy. But the area did attract some famous figures, from Mozart, who was welcomed here as a child during a tour of Europe, and Karl Marx, who lodged for a few years above what is now the well-known Quo Vadis restaurant in Dean Street, to such rock legends as Jimi Hendrix, Eric Clapton and the punk group the Sex Pistols. For a long time, Soho's prosperity came from its thriving sex trade, and the seedy clubs, bars and sex shops made the area an unwelcoming place for many Londoners and tourists alike. Today, however, the notorious red-light district of old has smartened up its act somewhat, and the area is now a vibrant mix of restaurants, boutiques, clubs and pubs.

Highlife and nightlife: Soho has had a reputation as a red-light district for over 200 years, with a dense concentration of porn and striptease establishments as well as prostitutes. Nowadays the sex industry is concentrated in just one small part of Soho, mainly around Berwick and Brewer Streets. The old, rather dubious clip joints have generally been pushed out by cocktail bars, cafés and night clubs.

CHINATOWN

Although the name might suggest otherwise, Chinatown is not a completely separate district with a Chinese populace but just a small corner of Soho around Lisle and Gerrard Streets. Soho has always been a destination for immigrants from around the world and the Chinese community began to establish itself here after World War II, over time bringing restaurants, exotic stores, and an intriguing touch of the Far East to the area, a move prompted by the growing English taste for Chinese food during the 1960s and 1970s. The success of the first restaurants attracted more Chinese from London's East End to try their luck here, while many brought their relatives from the former British colony of Hong Kong. The Chinese community expanded and with it grew its cultural confidence. Nowadays Chinatown is a firm part of multicultural London.

You could almost forget that this is London: fast-food stands, restaurants and supermarkets offer exotic dishes and ingredients that can usually only be found in a Chinese kitchen. The street signs are bilingual and the houses and shop fronts are festooned with Chinese decorations, especially during the Chinese New Year celebrations, which are one of the high points in London's festive calendar.

SHAFTESBURY AVENUE

Shaftesbury Avenue is a busy through road and consequently not the place to go for a peaceful stroll. When it is lit up in the evening, however, it is the centre of London's 'theatreland' and the heart of the West End, where a good number of the city's greatest stages are to be found. Most of the theatre buildings, including the Gielgud, the Apollo and the Lyric, are concentrated on the stretch that runs between Piccadilly Circus and Charing Cross Road. The Apollo and the Lyric, which today focuses on light comedies and musicals, although it opened in 1888 as an opera house, are now listed buildings. The Gielgud also originally opened as an opera house, but today specializes in serious drama. The Palace Theatre, which belongs to the musical mogul and composer Andrew Lloyd Webber, has the biggest auditorium of all the Shaftesbury Avenue theatres.

The Queen's Theatre (left) has seen many big stars tread its boards, including Alec Guinness and Kenneth Branagh. The emotive musical 'Les Misérables', based on Victor Hugo's novel, moved to the Queen's in 2004. Before that it had enjoyed an 18-year run at the Palace Theatre down the road, making it the longest-running musical in the West End. The Lyric Theatre (below) is the oldest theatre in the street.

LONDON'S WEST END THEATRES

At the heart of London's glittering West End lie 50 or so major theatres, many of them historic buildings dating back to Victorian or Edwardian times. Hand-in-hand with with the opulent, grand interiors typical of the period are the sometimes cramped conditions of the seating and the refreshment facilities, but the buildings' protected status makes modernization difficult. In order to survive financially, the majority of the commercial theatres, which are privately owned, are forced to concentrate on productions likely to attract full audiences – which is currently musicals. The non-commercial theatres such as the National Theatre, Royal Court and Shakespeare's Globe are assisted financially with state subsidies. They can accordingly be more adventurous, trying out new playwrights and controversial works. Ballet and opera are performed at the Coliseum, home of the English National Opera and the English National Ballet, and the Royal Opera House. The latter dates from the mid 19th century, but was substantially redesigned in the 1990s. Many plays are put on beyond the West End, sometimes in less orthodox venues such as small rooms above pubs. London's oldest theatrical venue is the Theatre Royal Drury Lane, on the site of a playhouse dating back to around 1662, though the present building dates from 1811.

The Garrick Theatre (below left) was named after the actor David Garrick (1717–79). The more traditional theatres have often retained their original interiors, such as the Coliseum (below right, top), the home stage of the English National Opera and the English National Ballet, and the Aldwych Theatre (below right, bottom). John Gay's 'Beggar's Opera' was premiered at the Haymarket Theatre (left) in 1729.

PICCADILLY CIRCUS

Five busy thoroughfares meet at Piccadilly Circus. The junction is considered to be the gateway to the amusements of the West End and Soho, making it an ever-popular tourist haunt. It's not exactly pretty, but it is always loud and noisy, and its reputation among tourists as the glittering focus of London's fantastic nightlife refuses to go away. The name Piccadilly Circus probably stems from the lace collars – or 'piccadills' – sold here in the 17th century.

From 1923, huge illuminated billboards were plastered across all sides of Piccadilly Circus, and when night fell their flashing bulbs spelt out the boundless promise of the consumerist society for all to see. The high price of advertising space, however, means that the giant signs are now limited to just one side of Piccadilly Circus. The Trocadero, once a music hall, has also moved with the times – it's now a massive shopping and entertainment complex.

The trickling fountain in the centre of the square was built for Lord Shaftesbury, the philanthropist, and is topped by a statue that raised a few contemporary eyebrows – it was naked (left). The discreet Victorians called it the 'Angel of Christian Charity', but Londoners have always cheerfully called it Eros. It is actually a representation of Anteros, the brother of Eros, the god of love.

FORTNUM & MASON

Fortnum & Mason is the epitome of the upper-class English department store. Founded in 1707, it has had a royal warrant for more than 150 years, and not just for the unsurpassed delicatessen which it sources from all over the world. This traditional store on Piccadilly was the first to import exotic provisions from the nascent British empire and also the first to produce ready-made snacks, such as game in aspic and soft biscuits, to be enjoyed on grand picnics. It was also a pioneer in the discovery of what was once a culinary novelty but has since become cheap and ubiquitous: tinned baked beans, produced by a certain Mr Heinz from America. There was even a service for explorers who wished to chart new territory but just couldn't do so without a supply of smoked salmon and champagne. Fortnum & Mason's selection of teas is renowned, as is its range of gift items and hampers for the smart set, the most exclusive category of which can cost as much as several thousand pounds. These days the store also sells other products, such as perfumes, candles, garden party requisites, clothes for the landed gentry, and exquisite tea services with cakestands for high tea. These are all of the highest quality, of course, and the prices are resolutely aimed at an upper-class clientele.

This smart store's window displays are among the most opulent and beautiful in London, while the interior reflects its luxurious elegance as well. The spectacular atrium was added only in 2007 after an expensive refurbishment about which the old customers are still in two minds. For many it seems to have lost some of its former charm, while others have praised the rejuvenation of a traditional store.

WHITEHALL / BANQUETING HOUSE

Whitehall is the seat of the British government's power, a magnificent boulevard leading northwest from the Houses of Parliament and lined by numerous administrative buildings, including the Ministries of Defence and Health, the Foreign Office and the Treasury. It was once the highway between the Palaces of Westminster and Whitehall. At its height, Whitehall was the finest palace in Europe; it was a royal palace from 1049, and in 1530 Henry VIII made it the sovereign's principal London residence. The palace burnt down in 1698, only the magnificent Banqueting House, added in 1622, surviving in its entirety. England's first neoclassical building, the Banqueting House was designed by Inigo Jones, who was inspired by the Venetian architect Palladio and brought Palladian architecture to England. It was the perfect setting for elegant court entertainments.

All that remains of the Palace of Whitehall, the two-storey Banqueting House (below right) was designed by Inigo Jones. Inside the building is a minstrels' gallery and a coffered ceiling painted by Rubens, depicting the 'Apotheosis of James I', commissioned by the latter's son, Charles I – who was executed in front of the building in 1649. Left: A painting by Canaletto with the Banqueting House in the background.

HORSE GUARDS PARADE

Every morning the Household Cavalry conduct the changing of the guard ceremony on Horse Guards Parade, a spectacle every bit as popular as the one held at Buckingham Palace. Horse Guards Parade, a square in Whitehall, has remained loyal to its history, with only a few exceptions. It was originally Henry VIII's tiltyard, but in 1755 a building and parade ground was constructed here for the royal guards and it has since functioned as the official entrance to the royal residences. Apart from the changing of the guard, various other ceremonies and events are held here, including the annual Trooping the Colour parade marking the Queen's official birthday, and in 2009 the polo world championship was held here for the first time. There is perhaps less pageantry associated with the plan to hold the 2012 Olympics beach volleyball competition here.

The Household Cavalry now only has ceremonial duties, even though it remains part of the British army. The changing of the guard takes place at 11.00 every morning (10.00 on Sundays), during which 12 mounted troopers dressed in traditional uniform ride up to Hyde Park barracks to relieve their predecessors. The horses are always black and of Irish stock, although the trumpeter's horse is a gray.

DOWNING STREET

No. 10 Downing Street hardly resembles the seat of power of a once mighty empire; it looks more like a typical Georgian terraced house, albeit quite an attractive one. In fact, the building comprises what were once three houses and now boasts 60 rooms. The somewhat plain façade may owe its origins to British democracy. In the 18th century it was the residence of the Prussian ambassador, one Count von Bothmer from Mecklenburg. After his death, it was requisitioned by the Hanoverian English king George II and handed over to Walpole, his First Minister, who is now considered to be the first Prime Minister of Great Britain. It has since been the official residence of the British prime minister, and this seemingly modest house, with the typical British 'bobby' standing on guard outside the door, is a high security area and not accessible to mere mortals.

THE PALACE OF WESTMINSTER

The equestrian statue of Richard the Lionheart (left) guards the palace façade. Westminster Hall (below left) dates back to 1097 and was once the largest hall in Europe. It is used for coronation banquets and for lying in state before royal burials, among other things. The Queen dons her robes of state in the Robing Room with its throne (below right, bottom) and then enters the Royal Gallery (below right, top) to open parliament.

THE HOUSE OF LORDS / THE HOUSE OF COMMONS

The House of Commons and the House of Lords have been located in the Palace of Westminster, or the Houses of Parliament, as it is also known, since the 16th century. The House of Lords once had far more power than the elected Commons, and the balance of power has only slowly been shifting since the 19th century. Nowadays the Lords, who include bishops and judges among their ranks, can only delay legislation, not prevent it being passed. The State Opening, the annual beginning of the parliamentary session, has been one of the most elaborate ceremonies in England for over 500 years. In full regalia, the Queen reads a speech written by the prime minister and the cabinet which outlines the government's plans to an audience that includes ambassadors, judges, dignitaries, and members of parliament in parliamentary dress or national costume.

All the greats of world politics have gone in and out of Downing Street, some finding a place in the annals of history and some being quickly forgotten. Here Gordon Brown, the British prime minister, is seen accompanying Barack Obama, the president of the USA, to greet the press outside 'Number Ten' – one of British politics' major photo opportunities, guaranteed a place on the the front cover of all the newspapers.

FIRST LORD of the TREASURY

THE PALACE OF WESTMINSTER

Staring at its reflection in the Thames, you could be forgiven for thinking that the neo-Gothic Westminster Palace – with Big Ben and its other characteristic towers – had stood here since the Middle Ages. There has indeed been a royal palace on this site since the 11th century, but the present building was constructed in the mid-19th century, after its predecessor was destroyed by fire. The only surviving sections of the medieval structure are the Jewel Tower – once King Edward III's treasure chamber and now home to a parliamentary museum – and Westminster Hall, which is now only used for ceremonial occasions. Like Westminster Abbey, the Palace of Westminster is a UNESCO World Heritage Site. It is the world's largest parliamentary building, with more than 1,100 rooms, 100 staircases, and 3 km (2 miles) of corridors. Both the upper and lower houses of Parliament sit within its walls.

Red versus green: the Lords debating chamber (below left and below right, top), where the State Opening takes place, has red benches, the more austere Commons chamber has green (left).
The seating plan in the Commons is prescribed: the party in government sits on one side and the opposition sit on the other. Below right, bottom: The shelves of the Lords' library are lined with mainly legal tomes.

WESTMINSTER ABBEY

It's not just its magnificent architecture that makes Westminster Abbey – or, to give it its official name, The Collegiate Church of St Peter, Westminster – such a unique place of worship. What is really impressive is the wealth of symbolic references contained in the fabric of the building. Almost every British monarch since William the Conqueror has been crowned at the abbey, in a ceremony traditionally performed by the Archbishop of Canterbury. Many were also laid to rest here, and their remains lie alongside numerous great historic figures, from writers and artists to scientists and politicians. Permission to be buried at the abbey is granted to only the greatest Britons. The building itself is a mix of architectural styles, the result of centuries of alterations. Taken as a whole, however, the church is still the finest example of English Gothic and the true jewel in London's crown.

The central nave of Westminster Abbey is rather narrow at only 10 metres (33 feet), but it is the highest in England, which only adds to its imposing effect. The abbey contains some of the finest surviving examples of medieval masonry, fortunately spared the depredations of the Dissolution of the Monasteries ordered by Henry VIII. Nowadays it serves as a museum, in addition to being a church.

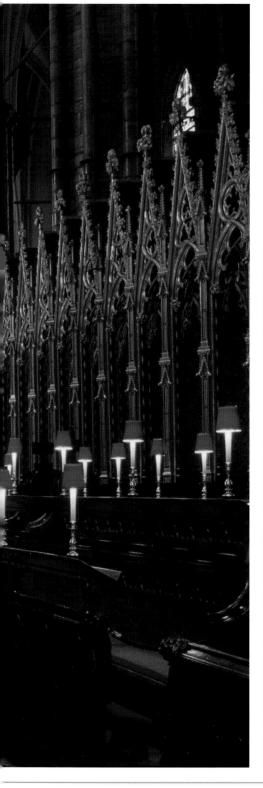

CHAPEL OF HENRY VII

The Lady Chapel, or Chapel of Henry VII, is considered to be the last great masterpiece of English medieval architecture. Built at the east end of Westminster Abbey between 1503 and 1519 by Henry VII, the first Tudor monarch, it is separated from the main nave by a flight of steps and bronze gates adorned with Tudor emblems. Henry and his consort, Elizabeth of York, lie buried behind the altar in a tomb designed by Pietro Torrigiano.

The most arresting detail of the chapel is the spectacular fan vaulting with carved pendants, created by talented but now long-forgotten stone masons. The walls are lined with statues of 95 saints and above these hang the standards of the members of the Order of the Bath, which was instituted here in 1725. This knighthood is a distinction awarded to prominent soldiers and civil servants, nowadays proposed by the prime minister.

The chapel is a royal vault, built principally for the Tudors: Mary I and Elizabeth I are buried in the north aisle. The tomb of Margaret Douglas, Countess of Lennox, commemorates a remarkable woman. By judiciously marrying off her son she ensured the accession of her grandson, the Scottish James VI, to the English throne as James I. Below: The vaulted roof with the standards of the Order of the Bath.

THE TOMBS OF WESTMINSTER ABBEY

The list of kings, queens, nobles, top politicians, scientists, writers, musicians, artists and dignitaries buried at Westminster Abbey is almost endless. Some – like England's great Queen Elizabeth I (d. 1603) – were given elaborate tombs, while others are commemorated with tasteful monuments or simple memorial stones. Edward the Confessor, responsible for the construction of Westminster Abbey, was the first king to be buried here. Every British monarch from Henry III (d. 1272) to George II (d. 1760) is also buried in Westminster Abbey, while numerous aristocrats, monks and other figures with connections to the abbey are buried in the churchyard outside. The poet Geoffrey Chaucer (who died around 1400) was the first literary figure to be buried at Westminster Abbey. Many other great playwrights, poets and authors are buried here, including Charles Dickens, Thomas Hardy and Ben Johnson, who was buried upright due to reduced circumstances at the time of his death. There are also memorials to other writers whose remains lie elsewhere, such as Oscar Wilde and William Shakespeare. In total, some 3,300 people are buried in the abbey and its grounds. Among the 600 memorials and monuments are the tombs of Sir Isaac Newton (d. 1722), Charles Darwin (d. 1882) and composer Handel (d. 1759).

Henry III, whose tomb is one of the oldest in the abbey (left), made Westminster the seat of government, introducing a 'parliament' of 15 nobles, and also extended the abbey as a shrine to Edward the Confessor. Eleanor of Castile (far left) married Henry's son, Edward I, and was considered a strong and intelligent woman. Below: The magnificent tomb of Queen Elizabeth I.

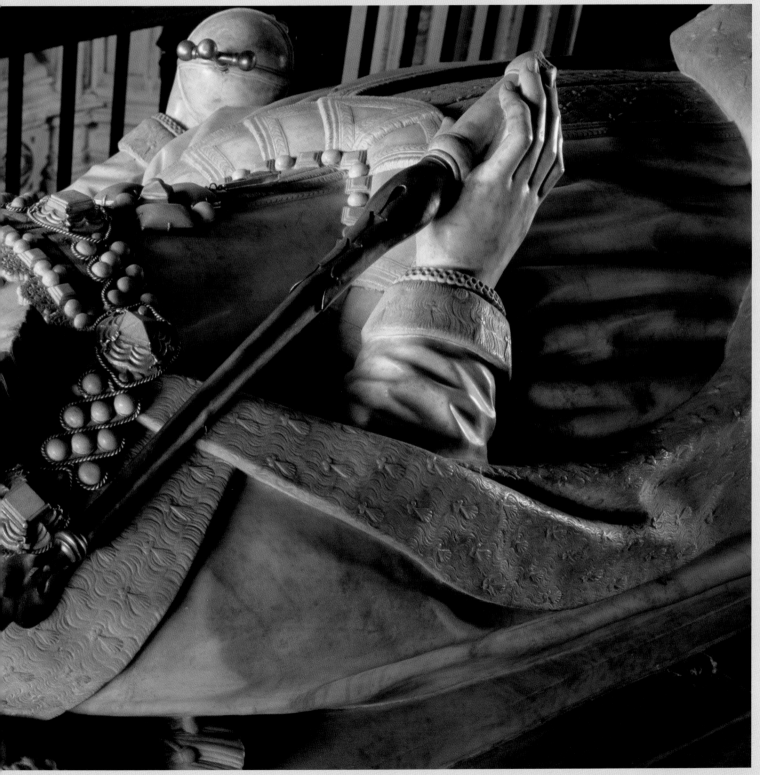

TATE BRITAIN

Tate Britain is a unique collection of British art from 1500 to the present day. Next to the neoclassical main entrance, the new Clore Gallery is home to the Tate's collection of paintings by the Romantic master painter William Turner. His memory lives on in the prestigious Turner Prize, awarded to a young British artist every year. The Tate's temporary exhibitions are also the cause of much sensation, often focusing not just on a single artist, but instead exploring all sorts of wider themes. Tate Britain was born as the National Gallery of British Art in 1897. It was popularly known as the Tate Gallery after its 19th-century millionaire benefactor Sir Henry Tate, who bequeathed not only his collection of contemporary art to the state, but also enough money to build a museum worthy of the collection's display. Tate Britain is now one of the four galleries across Britain collectively known as the Tate.

The mural 'History of the World 1997–2004' (below right, top) by Jeremy Deller, who won the Turner Prize in 2004 for his installation 'Memory Bucket'. Richard Deacon won the Turner Prize in 1987 – his works (below right, bottom) are abstract, often consisting of found materials. The exhibition 'Heaven and Earth' focused on landscape and movement and featured works by Richard Long (below left).

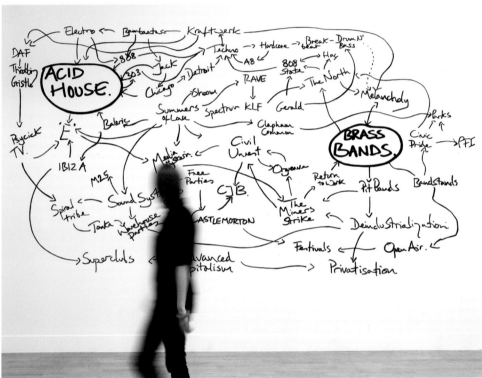

WESTMINSTER CATHEDRAL

Compared with the historically important and popular Westminster Abbey, Westminster Cathedral is not just an architectural surprise but an oasis of peace in the hustle and bustle of the city. It is the mother church of the Roman Catholic community in England and Wales and the metropolitan seat of the Archbishop of Westminster, who is usually also a cardinal. Construction of the cathedral began in 1895; it was only the second Catholic church to be built since the English Reformation in the 16th century. The interior is based on a Byzantine idiom, with striking, glittering mosaics, marble decoration – incorporating 125 different kinds of marble from 24 countries – and 14 stone reliefs by Eric Gill which depict the Stations of the Cross. The floors of the various chapels, with their beautiful themed patterns, are a true delight.

WESTMINSTER CATHEDRAL

The cathedral's architecture, with its red brick and white sandstone striping, is a trademark of this area of London. Neo-Byzantine associations are also unmistakable in the façade with its domes, balconies, arched windows, and an 83-metre (272-foot) high 'campanile' (left), as well as in the interior of the building. The cathedral boys' choir has found fame by specializing in Renaissance music.

BUCKINGHAM PALACE / VICTORIA MONUMENT

Buckingham Palace is the official weekday residence of the royal family. The royals abandon it in the summer, so during August and September the palace doors are thrown open and 19 of its rooms put on public display. The central core of this splendid palace dates back to 1705, when the building belonged to the Duke of Buckingham. In 1837, Queen Victoria decided that St James's Palace no longer measured up to the standards required of a royal residence, and moved into Buckingham Palace instead. By that time, the building had been restructured into a palace truly worthy of the name. Further modernization and improvement works continued until the beginning of the 20th century, culminating in the refacing of the building's eastern façade in 1913. On important state occasions, the royals appear on the balcony on this side of the building, graciously waving to the crowds below.

The Victoria Memorial, designed by Sir Aston Webb, was constructed in front of Buckingham Palace's main façade in 1911. It stands some 25 metres (82 feet) high and was fashioned from 2,300 tons of white marble. The statue of Queen Victoria looks down the Mall, while the memorial is topped with the figure of the goddess of victory. Left: A detail of the elegantly decorated palace gates.

THE ROYALS

The 11-hour-long coronation of Queen Elizabeth II was the first major event to be watched by millions of television viewers across Europe. Since then, the British royal family has lost none of its fascination. Stories and scandals involving the royals always get people talking – giving the tabloid press a circulation boost in the process. Events have certainly shaken the royal family's understanding of its place in British society, but the media is far from bringing down the House of Windsor. The Queen has combined her adherence to rigid protocol with increasing efforts to appear less aloof. An example of this was the decision to put part of the royal art collection on public display in the newly renovated Queen's Gallery. Located in the south wing of Buckingham Palace, this rich collection includes works by Rembrandt, van Dyck, Canaletto, Titian and Vermeer. In summer, some of the palace's living areas are also opened to visitors, with a collection of the Queen's dresses on display. This charm offensive seems to have worked, and top fashion magazine 'Vogue' declared Queen Elizabeth one of the world's 50 most glamorous women. That said, the focus of press interest is increasingly on Prince William and his brother Harry, Prince Charles' sons from his marriage to Diana, Princess of Wales, who tragically died in a car crash in Paris in 1997.

The Queen with her eternal successor, Prince Charles (far left), and her grandsons, Princes William and Harry (left and below left). Even the Windsors have not been spared the modern fashion for patchwork families – Prince Charles and his wife Camilla (below right) are both on their second marriages. Princess Anne, the Queen's daughter (third from left) has also married twice.

CHANGING THE GUARD

At 11.30 every morning from May to July (otherwise every second day), one of London's most popular spectacles takes place at Buckingham Palace: Changing the Guard. The old guard detail exchanges duty with the new guard in the square in front of the palace gates in a 45-minute ceremony with much pomp and circumstance, to the accompaniment of a military band who play a selection of music from rousing traditional marches to themes from films and musicals, and even pop songs. The soldiers are drawn from one of the five Foot Guard regiments of the British army: the Scots Guards, the Irish Guards, the Welsh Guards, the Grenadier Guards and the Coldstream Guards, who all wear the same red jackets and bearskins but are distinguished by their collar insignia, the arrangement of the buttons on the their uniform jackets, and the colour and position of the plume on their caps. The troops are all members of the British army and perform normal military service. They wear traditional uniforms at the palace but the rifles they carry are real – the guard duty is taken very seriously. When the Queen is in residence at the palace four soldiers will be posted at the gates, otherwise there are only two. The guard is also changed in a similar ceremony at Windsor Castle.

CHANGING THE GUARD

The soldiers in their bearskins have long since retreated behind the gates of Buckingham Palace rather than standing guard in front of them, as tourists were bothering them too often. A lone soldier is posted in front of St James Palace in Pall Mall (below left) so visitors can take pictures. The ceremonial Changing the Guard is always performed to a musical accompaniment (below right).

BELGRAVIA

Belgravia is London's smartest district by some margin, a green and pleasant area with white townhouses and some of the city's richest inhabitants. Little wonder: a house in this vicinity costs around £15m and even an apartment costs several million. The area was developed at the beginning of the 19th century on land belonging to Richard Grosvenor, the second Marquess of Westminster. It has always been the exclusive residential area it remains to this day: Margaret Thatcher, the former prime minister, lives here, as do the art collector Charles Saatchi and the actress Joan Collins, and a number of embassies are located on up-market Belgrave Square. Eaton Square is the biggest square, although many of the townhouses here have now been divided up into apartments. The pretty façades and cobbled side streets are extremely picturesque.

The Belgrave Gallery (left) is as exclusive as its location, selling not only works by the likes of such masters as Picasso, Rembrandt and Roy Lichtenstein, but also drawings by Nelson Mandela and paintings by Prince Charles. Some of the finest house façades are to be seen on Upper Belgrave Street (below right); Belgravia is dotted with a number of pubs and street cafés (below left).

HYDE PARK

Pink Floyd and the Rolling Stones are just two of the big rock bands to have performed in Hyde Park; other musicians who have drawn huge audiences here, however inclement the weather, include the great tenor Luciano Pavarotti. There was a time when gentlemen came here to duel at dawn, and robbers and pickpockets stalked their victims, but life in this tranquil London park now moves at a rather more gentle pace. Covering an area of some 142 ha (351 acres), Hyde Park is truly a park for the people, the first royal park to be made accessible to the general public, and at its north-east corner is the only public place where anyone can openly speak their mind to the people, as long as the speech is considered lawful. Speakers' Corner is a British institution, a place where the right of anyone to speak has been enshrined in law since the Parks Regulation Act of 1872.

Forming a counterpart to Marble Arch on the north side of Hyde Park, Wellington Arch, built in 1830, is located on the south side of the park, not far from Speakers' Corner (below right). It is topped with a 'quadriga', the largest bronze sculpture in Great Britain. The park is so big that everyone can find a quiet corner (left), and is at its most beautiful in the early morning (below left).

TIME FOR TEA

Tea at The Ritz is a London institution, and mere passers-by cannot simply breeze in for a quick cup of tea and a cake. Long considered the ultimate in style, The Ritz gave rise to the word 'ritzy' to describe high-class living. It was opened in 1906 by Swiss hotelier César Ritz, who hired chef Auguste Escoffier to please wealthy palates. At The Ritz's splendid Palm Court tearoom the hotel's refined guests, who are expected to adhere to a formal dress code, are treated to an array of classic afternoon tea delicacies. The finest tea – often one of the hotel's unique blends – is served in silver teapots and sipped from the best porcelain with milk and sugar to taste. It's generally accompanied by an array of tasty morsels, in particular little bite-size sandwiches, crusts removed, filled with egg and cress, fish paste, smoked salmon, ham or wafer-thin slices of cucumber. Temptingly indulgent little cakes are also part of the experience, from a slice of pink and yellow Battenberg cake, to fruit cakes, lemon cakes and – of course – scones with jam and clotted cream (a thick cream made from scalded milk). Though different establishments put their own twist on afternoon tea, they would be doing it a disservice were they to omit any of the key components listed above. And that – as any true lady or gentleman will tell you – just would not do at all.

TIME FOR TEA

The Ritz's exquisite Palm Court (below left) demands formal dress from its patrons. Ladies often wear hats when taking afternoon tea here, even if the nod to the traditional atmosphere sometimes borders on the ironic (below right). Every now and then there is even a tea dance (left), which remains a distinctly English and stately affair – much like the attentive but very formal staff (far left).

Oxford Street is heaven on earth for shopaholics: the 300 boutiques and department stores spread along its 2.5 kilometres (a mile and a half) stock everything the heart could desire. Considered Europe's greatest shopping street, many British labels have their headquarters here, offering a mix of smart designer wear and popular high street fashion. Among the big names is the House of Fraser (below left, top), a fashion department store stocking everything from Armani and Moschino to Wrangler for the fashion-conscious Londoner, and the American fashion chain Gap (below left, bottom), which has its British headquarters here. Selfridges, the second-largest department store in the UK after Harrods, sells similarly up-market wares. Marks & Spencer has its flagship store here too, with a huge food hall that attracts people in a hurry on their lunch break.

Oxford Street, a street off smart Regent Street (left), is famous for its Christmas illuminations, which are always turned on by a celebrity in a blaze of publicity. The Selfridges department store regularly organizes exhibitions, performances and advertising events, such as when the lingerie brand Agent Provocateur had the artist 'Jacques le Trompe' paint a naked model in the shop window.

LONDON CABS AND BUSES

If London is to appear as the backdrop for a film scene, you need only one of three things in the establishing shot: Big Ben, a black cab, or a red double-decker bus, all of which are icons of the British capital. The original 1950s red double-decker, the Routemaster, was initially produced exclusively for London. Its design was unmistakable and practically ideal for a big city: the entrance was via an open platform at the back of the bus, making it possible to jump on and off between official stops in heavy traffic. The disadvantages, however, were that it required a crew of two, a driver and a conductor, and that it was unsuitable for disabled access. The traditional Routemaster has therefore been gradually replaced by low-level buses, some of which are 'bendy' buses and some modern double-deckers. Both of these are more practical in design and more economical to run, but are decidedly less popular with tradition-conscious Londoners. The Routemaster still runs on two historic routes, the number 9 from the Royal Albert Hall via Piccadilly Circus to Aldwych, and the number 15 from Trafalgar Square via Fleet Street to Tower Hill. Routemasters are due to be reintroduced to London's streets in the next few years, albeit in a modernized incarnation.

LONDON CABS AND BUSES

Black cabs, the typical London taxis, were also specially designed for the capital. They have a fantastically tight turning circle, plenty of space for passengers and their shopping bags, and a separate compartment for the driver. They are no longer all black, however, coming in a variety of shades, and the bodywork design has been modernized over the years. Below: A double-decker races over Westminster Bridge.

MADAME TUSSAUDS

Mere mortals rarely get the chance to come face to face with world-famous celebrities, but in the galleries of Madame Tussauds those very same stars are almost near enough to touch. Most of the famous faces of modern history are represented, from pop idols to sporting champions and politicians. Not that all the faces are friendly – serial killers, tyrants and gangsters are all here too, presented in a wide array of thematic displays. Born Marie Grosholtz in 18th-century Strasbourg, Tussaud started her collection in the French Revolution when she was charged with making death masks for the victims of the guillotine. Years later, she put her collection of waxworks on public display in London's Baker Street, from where it was moved in the 19th century to its current home on Marylebone Road. The collection is updated regularly, with new figures replacing those relegated to the storeroom.

Unlike contemporary figures, those from history don't need updating, just retouching every now and again. The widowed Queen Victoria (below right, top) has found immortality in old age, as has Pablo Picasso (left), but, for the moment at least, modern pop icons such as the Beatles (below right, bottom), Kylie Minogue (below left) and Madonna (far left) are permitted to remain young, thin and beautiful.

THE UNDERGROUND

The underground railway network, known as the 'Tube' because of the shape of its tunnels, is the quickest way of getting around London, although not necessarily the most comfortable, especially on certain stretches at peak times on workdays in the heat of summer. The Tube carries a billion passengers a year across London and things can get a bit crowded at rush hour, to the extent that sometimes platforms have to be closed or trains just drive straight through stations without stopping. The Tube is the oldest underground rail system in the world; the first line between Paddington and Hammersmith was opened as far back as 1863 and in 1890 electrically powered trains were introduced, another first for the city. There are currently 11 lines in service; a twelfth, the East London Line, was discontinued in 2007 for alterations but is due to reopen in 2010. The lines are colour-coded to help passengers get around – the longest is the Central Line (red), at 74 kilometres (46 miles). There is a total of 270 stations on 400 kilometres (248 miles) of track, making it the largest underground network in the world, and further extensions are planned. The trains don't just travel underground – 55% of the track, which reaches far beyond London's city boundaries, runs overground.

THE UNDERGROUND

'Mind the gap!' – a warning about the space between the train and the platform – is often announced as the train approaches and has become much imitated by Londoners. It does make good sense, though, as some of the older stations have large gaps, particularly on curved platforms. The Tube logo, a red circle with a blue cross-bar, is recognized all over the world and has become one of London's trademarks.

KENSINGTON AND CHELSEA

Kensington, Chelsea and the slightly less exclusive Notting Hill are among the most expensive places to live in the entire United Kingdom, and their well-maintained houses make highly desirable homes for anyone rich enough to afford them. Kensington Gardens – separated from Hyde Park only by the Serpentine lake – lies at the heart of the area. The park is surrounded by grand embassies, top-flight museums and Kensington Palace, whose imposing structure is a popular attraction for followers of the royal family. Kensington High Street, meanwhile, is one of London's finest shopping streets.

Brompton Road in fashionable Knightsbridge is lined with smart restaurants, five-star hotels and up-market shops. But the jewel in the crown is Harrods – probably the most famous department store in the world (below), where the rich and famous do their shopping – or have it done.

SLOANE STREET / HARVEY NICHOLS

Sloane Street would win hands down the title of 'London's most exclusive shopping street'. It is so exclusive that it has given its name to a small, equally exclusive social group known as 'Sloane Rangers' – wealthy young members of the upper class with the means to support a privileged lifestyle and united by a private education. The street is the dividing line between the smart suburbs of Knightsbridge, Belgravia and Chelsea, and caters to the needs of well-off local residents, among whom are many of the super-rich from the Arabic states; just one family from Dubai has bought up large sections of the west side of Sloane Street. All the top brands and designers can be found here, including the up-market department store Harvey Nichols – less well known than Harrods but often more expensive and attracting a younger and very fashion-conscious clientele.

'Harvey Nicks' (far left), as the exclusive store is affectionately known, doesn't just sell trendy fashion, there is a restaurant, a café and a cool bar on the fifth floor (left). There are plenty of opportunities for 'Sloanes' to spend lots of money on luxury designers, whether at Emilio Pucci's (below left), the lingerie shop La Perla (below right, bottom), or on clothes bearing the Alberta Ferretti label (below right, top).

HARRODS

Never make the mistake of confusing Harrods with just any old department store. This temple of consumerism is a British institution. The store, standing on a 1.8-ha (4.5-acre) plot, has sales floors covering some 93,000 sq m (111,200 sq yards), with 330 departments, 28 restaurants, 5,000 employees, and up to 300,000 customers passing through its doors every day. All this makes Harrods the biggest department store in Europe, and one of the biggest in the world. The store's motto is 'Omnia Omnibus Ubique' ('all things for all people, everywhere'), and it certainly lives up to its promise. Now part of a larger business empire, Harrods was founded by Charles Henry Harrod in 1834 and started life as a grocery and tea merchants based in London's East End, moving to the more exclusive Knightsbridge 15 years later. The current building dates from 1905 after its predecessor was destroyed by fire.

Harrods takes up a whole city block and is surrounded by up-market shops (far left), although these pale in comparison with the department store's opulent excesses. The range of products is overwhelming, as is the luxurious presentation and the store's impressive architecture (left and below right). The food hall is heaven on earth for gourmets, with lots of 'snack bars' (below left).

THE SAATCHI GALLERY

The Saatchi Gallery specializes in contemporary art, often showing exhibitions and artists that would make the Tate Modern feel envious; as a privately owned gallery, the Saatchi is not subject to any restrictions, whether financial or otherwise. Founded in 1985 by Charles Saatchi, a co-founder of the eponymous globally successful advertising agency and an avid art collector, the gallery concentrates less on current works created by famous names and more on younger and often unknown artists. Its themed exhibitions have often caused controversy, such as 1997's aptly named 'Sensation' with works by young British artists, which also caused a storm in both Berlin and New York. Although the reception for exhibitions at the gallery's new site in Chelsea has been somewhat calmer, the works on display are no less exciting and innovative.

The new gallery space is in the Duke of York's barracks on the King's Road (left). Will Ryman is one of Saatchi's 'discoveries' and the artist's sculpture 'Bed' (below left) perhaps contains suggestions of his past in the theatre. The new gallery was opened in 2008 with a show of works by Chinese artists, including giant sculptures by Xiang Jing (below right, top) and Warhol-like portraits by Feng Zheng-ji (below right, bottom).

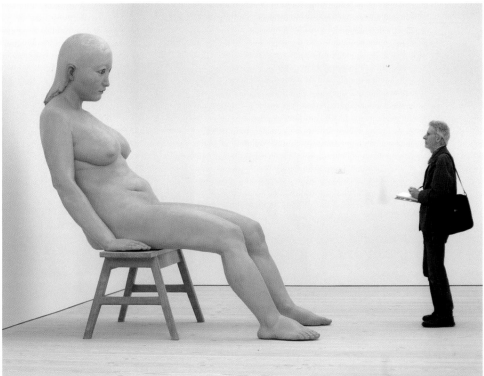

SLOANE SQUARE / KING'S ROAD

Until 1830 the King's Road was a private royal thoroughfare leading to Hampton Court, and its eastern end, reaching as far as Sloane Square, is still lined with plenty of fine houses. Nowadays it serves as a shopping street in the heart of fashionable Chelsea, with many boutiques, restaurants and cafés. However, its reputation was made as the scene of fashion revolutions which began in London and went on to conquer the world, with influences that are still felt today. Mary Quant's boutique here, Bazaar, was where mini-skirts, hot pants and thick make up first became popular in the 1960s, and a decade later Vivienne Westwood and Malcolm McLaren, the manager of the Sex Pistols, were to open a boutique called Sex, selling punk fashion and outrageous designer outfits. The boutique is still there, but has a rather less controversial name, World's End.

Sloane Square, with its cafés and restaurants (below left), connects the King's Road and smart Sloane Street (far left). Now dominated by conventional entertainment (left) and the mainstream rather than by innovation, the once revolutionary King's Road seems much milder and more elegant (below left). Some quirky and of course expensive fashion (below right) is still to be found here, however.

THE ROYAL HOSPITAL CHELSEA

The Royal Hospital of Chelsea is a typically British institution, allowing the heroes of a British Empire that once ruled the world to grow old in dignity; not all are admitted, however, as the rules are still very strict. Apart from age, length of service and rank, only soldiers without any family or other ties who fulfil the stringent formal requirements are admitted. Servicewomen only began to be admitted recently, housed separately from the men.

The house and its strict regulations were established by King Charles II in 1682 and the architect employed to undertake the design of the building was Christopher Wren, who took his inspiration from the Hôpital des Invalides in Paris. The grounds of the Royal Hospital have also found a popular civilian use as the site of Europe's most famous annual garden exhibition, the Royal Horticultural Society's Chelsea Flower Show.

The statue of Charles II in the inner courtyard portrays him as a Roman general (left). The Great Hall is one of the most beautiful spaces (below left) and was the veterans' dining hall until the 19th century. Each of the 16 tables was set for two warrant officers, two sergeants and 21 privates. The first televised church service in Great Britain was broadcast from the chapel (below right).

THE VICTORIA AND ALBERT MUSEUM

Named after Queen Victoria and her husband Prince Albert, the V&A (for short) and its vast building are a showcase for around 4.5 million valuable examples of craft and design from Europe, North America, Asia and North Africa, spanning a period from some 5,000 years ago right up to the present day. As if the geographic and historic breadth of the museum's exhibits were not impressive enough, the collection also encompasses the entire gamut of creative design, from sculpture, painting, drawing and photography to glasswork, porcelain and ceramics, furniture, toys, clothing and jewelry. This is the biggest collection of its kind in the world. It all started after the Great Exhibition of 1851, at which some of the more unusual exhibits were acquired. The collection quickly grew, and in 1899 Queen Victoria laid the foundation stone of the V&A's current building.

The museum is also a delight to behold from the outside (far left), creating a lavish setting for the collection. The great Cast Court (left) houses a collection of reproductions of European original masterpieces, such as Trajan's Column. There are also original sculptures (below right and below left, top), from busts to groups of figures. One of the prized exhibits is the State Coach (below left, bottom).

THE NATURAL HISTORY MUSEUM

Over and above its size and the scope of its collection, you could be forgiven for thinking that there is little to distinguish the Natural History Museum from its counterparts elsewhere. Like them, it was born of the 19th-century fascination with all creatures great and small – be they stuffed, preserved, a skeleton, or a model. It is a preoccupation from which the museum continues to thrive, but delve a little deeper and it soon becomes apparent that this museum is truly without comparison, a treasure trove of over 70 million specimens that document the complete history of the natural world. The collections of preserved specimens are in the main part of the museum, along with the newly enlarged Darwin Centre, a new phase of which opens soon, which tells the story of evolution. The amazing Earth Galleries, meanwhile, provide a fascinating insight into the geological history of our planet.

The museum building's steel frame was very innovative in its day, although the Victorian façade and atmosphere are definitely of their time (left). Despite the modern exhibitions, the classic exhibits are still the highlights of the museum, including dinosaur skeletons (below left) as well as stuffed animals (below right, bottom), and models of skeletons of prehistoric creatures (below right, top).

THE SCIENCE MUSEUM

Why? How come? What for? Questions that were often answered unsatisfactorily in school are addressed here in a manner that is very comprehensive and engaging. The Science Museum is one of the most advanced and innovative of its kind and there is hardly a branch of early or modern science that is not examined and presented in an exciting way. More than 300,000 exhibits are distributed across five floors, from microchips to entire planes, with many interactive displays. There is an Imax 3-D cinema with wrap-around sound for close encounters with the natural world and a library of associated literature. The museum also takes pains to ensure that visitors consider and explore the influence modern science has had on both people and the environment; the 'Talking Points' are works of art in the basement intended to stimulate thought and discussion.

The new Wellcome Wing (below left), named after the collector Sir Henry Wellcome, leads the world in the presentation of modern science and technology. The mighty Corliss steam engine is located in the East Hall (far left). The command module from Apollo 10 (left) is a big draw, as is the racing car (below right, top). The interactive launchpad gallery is not just for children (below right, bottom).

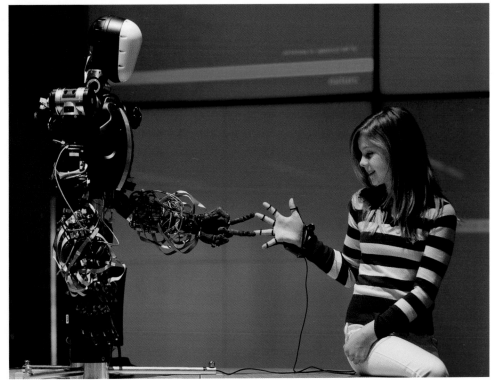

THE ROYAL ALBERT HALL

The Royal Albert Hall's huge, domed roof marks the heart of an area often termed the Albertopolis – named after Queen Victoria's husband, Prince Albert, in whose memory the widowed queen dedicated numerous cultural institutions in this part of London. Opened in 1871, the circular design of the Albert Hall is borrowed from ancient Roman arenas. The organ, which dominates the stage area, has nearly 10,000 pipes and is one of the largest in the country. Some of the world's most famous classical concerts – as well as many of the greatest pop and rock performances – have taken place on the stage below. In 1963, the Beatles and the Rolling Stones performed their only joint concert here. From Pink Floyd to Abba, many acts have played this venerable hall, which has also hosted tennis tournaments, conferences, award ceremonies and all manner of charity galas.

The circular form of the Royal Albert Hall is unmistakable (left and below left). The BBC promenade concerts, known as the Proms, are held here each evening over an eight-week period in summer (below right, bottom). The climax is the final concert, the 'Last Night of the Proms', when even the most retiring Brits literally show their colours and enthusiastically sing along (below right, top).

KENSINGTON GARDENS / PRINCE ALBERT MEMORIAL

Set in 111 ha (274 acres), Kensington Gardens was once the garden of Kensington Palace, and its landscaping is more formal than that of nearby Hyde Park. It is especially popular with children, who find plenty to keep them occupied within the confines of the well-tended park. In the east, not far from the Serpentine lake, stands the enchanting Peter Pan statue – a tribute to the famous fictional hero. The Diana Memorial Playground lies to the west – home to an adventure playground, a pirate ship and Indian tepees. For adults, the Serpentine Gallery – along with the park itself – is the biggest attraction. This 1930s tea pavilion is the venue for changing exhibitions of contemporary art, and the gallery's summer pavilion – created anew each year by a different leading architect – is a work of art in itself. Nearby, the Diana Memorial Fountain is a reminder of the late princess's connection to Kensington.

In 1876, after years of mourning, Queen Victoria dedicated a magnificent monument to the memory of her husband, Prince Albert, who had died unexpectedly young. The rich figuration and the lavish, almost kitschy, ornamentation of the Prince Albert Memorial (left) on the south side of Kensington Gardens represents the apotheosis of Victorian taste. Below: Kensington Palace's sunken garden.

KENSINGTON PALACE

The most famous recent resident of Kensington Palace was Princess Diana, who lived here with her sons William and Harry from 1981 to her death in 1997. The palace has been used as a royal residence since the 17th century, and in the course of time such architects as Christopher Wren have extended it from the original 'simple house' to an attractive palace. Other illustrious residents have included Queen Victoria, who was born here, and later Princess Margaret, the present Queen's late sister. Some of the apartments are the residences of minor royalty even today, although not on a permanent basis. The official state rooms are open to the public and one of the main attractions in the palace is a collection of ceremonial royal robes from the 18th to the 20th centuries, along with a collection of gowns and memorabilia belonging to Princess Diana.

As word spread of the untimely death of Princess Diana in 1997, the imposing gates of Kensington Palace were soon swathed in flowers. It was estimated that more than a million wreaths overflowed into Kensington Gardens and the palace is a shrine for Diana fans even today. Some of the rooms in Kensington Palace can be hired for private functions such as corporate events or weddings.

DIANA

Beautiful, elegant, glamorous, yet tragic – Diana, Princess of Wales, is as much a media icon in death as she was in life. One of the 20th century's most notable examples of the cult of celebrity, she became the most photographed woman on the planet, and pictures of her continue to fill the pages of the world's celebrity magazines. In 1997, when Diana – ex-wife of the heir to the throne, Prince Charles, and mother of the next in line, Prince William – was killed in a car crash in Paris, her death was greeted in Britain by unprecedented mass mourning. The then prime minister, Tony Blair, captured the mood of the nation when he described her as the 'people's princess', the queen of hearts. Numerous memorials have since been erected in her memory – her grave at her family home in Althorp has been turned into a shrine, and there is also a memorial fountain in Hyde Park and the Diana Memorial Playground in Kensington Gardens. But by far the most interesting memorial is the one at Kensington Palace, the Princess of Wales' last home. Here, alongside extensive audio-visual displays and a collection of memorabilia, some of Diana's elegant gowns have been put on display. Diana was a fashion-conscious princess, and most of the garments on show here were created specifically for her by Britain's top designers.

Victor Edelstein

The 11-kilometre (7-mile) long Memorial Walk links sites connected with Diana and is marked with metal plaques (left). Mohamed Al-Fayed, the father of Dodi, who died alongside Diana in Paris, built a shrine in the Harrods department store after their death (below left, top). The memorial to Diana exhibits not only photos of her, but also a selection of her dresses (below left, bottom).

NOTTING HILL / PORTOBELLO ROAD MARKET

Up until a few decades ago, Notting Hill was seen as a faded blot on the upper-class Kensington cityscape. It was a hotbed of social tension, and the scene, in 1958, of Britain's first race riots. At the time, most of the area's residents were of Afro-Caribbean origin, and it was these residents who, in the years after the racial clashes, started the Notting Hill Carnival – now one of London's brightest and best-known events. Notting Hill is still not exactly beautiful, but it is always exciting. The process of 'gentrification' – meaning not just the redevelopment and general tidying up of an area, but above all the influx of affluent young residents – has really had a dramatic impact on the face of Notting Hill. It has also seen prices soar. Portobello Road, for example – the heart of Notting Hill – boasts one of London's best markets, but it is now rarely the place to snap up a good bargain.

The Portobello Road lies in the heart of Notting Hill, and its innumerable shops, selling almost everything from junk to clothes, attract visitors even when the famous market is not on (far left, below left, and below right, top). Westbourne Grove, a smarter and rather less Bohemian side street, has several agreeable pubs (left). The police maintain order during the carnival (below right, bottom).

THE NOTTING HILL CARNIVAL

Carnival in Rio might hit the headlines and make you feel like buying a plane ticket, but London's Notting Hill Carnival is also in the running. Admittedly the English weather can rarely compete with that of Brazil, even though the event is held in August, but London's Afro-Caribbean celebration is just as lively and colourful. The whole event lasts for three days and the main procession, held on the bank holiday Monday, follows a 5-kilometre (3-mile) route. The carnival begins on Saturday evening with a steel band competition which since 2007 has been held in Hyde Park. Sunday is reserved for children, who have their own parade and seem to enjoy it just as much as the adults. The event has come to attract upwards of two million visitors and is a showcase of multi-cultural London, although this was not always the case; it was initially just a local event until the infamous 1958 Notting Hill race riots. The parade has only been held since 1965 and has not always been trouble-free – there used to be regular violent confrontations between predominantly Afro-Caribbean youths and the police. Nowadays, however, apart from the odd pickpocket and mild skirmish, the carnival is not only considerably more peaceful, it is a major London tourist attraction – so who needs Rio?

Soca and calypso, reggae, steel bands, and the most up-to-date pop music blast out from the carnival floats, people dance wherever there is room, and the streets are lined with snack stalls selling Caribbean food, but the focus is on the exciting costumes which individual groups have been working on for months. The brighter and quirkier the costume the better seems to be the motto.

NORTH LONDON

No other part of inner London is as diverse as this area. Bloomsbury, one of central London's greener residential areas, and parts of the area south of Regent's Park together form the main academic district, home to numerous university colleges and the world-famous British Museum. Camden Town is a more down-market area that has been adopted by the city's student fraternity, evidenced by the many alternative bars and venues. Refined and elegant, Regent's Park is surrounded by fine terraced townhouses designed by John Nash, the eminent architect responsible for much of Regency London.

Not so much beautiful as beautifully varied: Camden Town is a lively district with a market near Camden Lock that is famed throughout London. Boat trips run from Camden Lock to London Zoo and beyond to Paddington, offering a pleasant change from the bustle of the market.

SHRI SWAMINARAYAN MANDIR

India in London: this Hindu temple located in the suburb of Brent seems like a tiny splash of sub-continental brilliance in the English capital's grey sea of houses. It is completely authentic – the old tradition of avoiding metal fittings has been observed throughout the building and only lime-stone, granite and marble have been used, some of which was sent over to India so it could be intricately carved with traditional patterns and then returned. Topped with seven gold-tipped towers and five domes, it is Great Britain's first authentic Hindu temple and the largest outside India. Under each tower there is a shrine to a different god. Unlike many temples in India, the temple itself and the permanent exhibition 'Understanding Hinduism' located in the nearby cultural centre is open to non-believers and fol-lowers of all religions.

The largest ethnic 'minority' in London, with about half a million members, comes from India; many of these are the Hindus who independently financed and built the Shri Swaminarayan Temple. 'Mandir' is the Sanskrit word for 'sanctum' or 'place of meditation and prayer'. Ceremonies are held here every day honouring the Bhagwan Swaminarayan, who founded a modern sect of Hinduism in about 1800.

WEMBLEY STADIUM

Wembley Stadium, located in north-west London, is not just any stadium, it's a legend. England beat West Germany 4:2 here in the 1966 FIFA World Cup final and it was also the scene of the biggest concert of all time: the 1985 charity fundraiser Live Aid was not simply a rock gig featuring the biggest stars of the time, it was also viewed on television by some 1.4 billion people in 170 countries. The stadium was first opened as the Empire Stadium in 1924 and was closed in 2000. It was demolished in 2003 to make way for the current building, which was finally completed in 2007. Its 90,000 seats make it the second-largest stadium in Europe after the Camp Nou in Barcelona. Besides football, rugby matches and large rock concerts are also held here. The new national stadium, with its famous arch replacing the old building's two towers, is the pride of England.

WEMBLEY STADIUM

Kicking a ball around is an age-old sport, but the regulations for the modern game of football were only set down in England in the 19th century. Football is a national sport and international matches especially are followed by fans with unbridled national pride – they'll go to any lengths, even sporting a painted face and matching wig (left). Wembley Stadium's famous arch is 133 metres (437 feet) high (below).

HOOVER BUILDING

At night – or at least until 22.00 – the magnificent Hoover Building is bathed in fluorescent light like some extra-terrestrial apparition. During the day, the blinding white of its resplendently beautiful architecture makes it look more like a 1930s film set than a factory or office block. This art deco building, located on the A40 on the western edge of London, was designed by Wallis, Gilbert & Partners and built in 1935 as the headquarters of the UK branch of Hoover, the American vacuum cleaner company. 'Snowcrete' – white Portland cement, which retains its dazzling brightness – was used as a building material, and the painted fayence tiles that accentuate the building, along with its huge windows, give the impression that there is one gigantic hall hidden behind them; in fact there are several floors. Unique in London, the building has been listed since the 1980s.

In 1989, the supermarket chain Tesco bought
the partly derelict Hoover Building and carefully
restored it in cooperation with English Heritage.
The façade of the building was left unchanged,
but a new Tesco supermarket was constructed
behind it (left), whose façade is vaguely reminiscent of the original building's art deco style but
whose interior is as contemporary as any other
of the chain's stores.

BRITISH MUSEUM

Of Scottish and Irish descent, Sir Hans Sloane was a passionate collector of scientific specimens since childhood. Upon his death, Sloane bequeathed his entire collection – comprising over 70,000 items – to King George II for the nation. In 1753, this collection became the foundation of a museum that was the first of its kind anywhere in the world, containing objects from every academic field and every country. Today, the museum's holdings encompass millions of items and include some of the world's most famous treasures, like the Elgin Marbles from the Acropolis in Athens and the Rosetta Stone. The museum had already outgrown its original premises by the 19th century, and the current building dates from 1825. It boasts an imposing neoclassical façade, and has recently been made even more impressive by the addition of Sir Norman Foster's glass roof over the Great Court.

The great courtyard (left) is the largest roofed square in Europe. The museum is principally famous for its collection of Egyptian mummies (below right, bottom). These giant sculptures of gods and pharaohs (below left) are from Egyptian tombs. Among the most valuable exhibits are the controversial 'Elgin Marbles' – friezes and sculptures from the Parthenon temple at the Acropolis in Athens (below right, top).

THE BRITISH MUSEUM READING ROOM

The circular Reading Room lies at the centre of the Great Court. It used to be the British Library's main reading room, but this was moved to a new building at St Pancras. It was built in 1857 and for many years was only accessible to registered researchers, some more notable of whom included Lenin, Mahatma Ghandi, George Bernard Shaw and George Orwell. Karl Marx wrote part of his great work, 'Das Kapital', here. After careful restoration by the architect Norman Foster, when the magnificent interior of the dome was repaired, the Reading Room was opened to the general public for the first time in 2000. There is a modern information centre and some 25,000 books and other items of printed matter concerning the world cultures represented in the museum are available. The Reading Room is also being used as a temporary exhibition space until 2012.

The dome, modelled after the Pantheon in Rome, consists of a metal frame with a kind of papier-mâché cladding which has been restored to its former beauty in blue, cream and gold during the restoration work. The shelves are also made of metal in order to take the weight of the books. The whole room has a floor area of 1,651 square metres (17,770 square feet) and uses only low-heat and low-energy lighting.

THE BRITISH LIBRARY

The 625 kilometres (388 miles) of shelving at the British Library increase by 12 kilometres (7 miles) each year. The library holds printed and handwritten documents from every historical period, including an original copy of the Magna Carta and two Gutenberg Bibles. These, together with an audio collection of some three million recordings, help make the British Library one of the world's most important archives. The library, situated between King's Cross and Euston stations, has occupied its modern premises since 1998. The library itself is only open to holders of a reading pass, but some of its treasures are displayed in a public gallery. Among its unique documents are Captain Cook's journal, Charlotte Brontë's 'Jane Eyre', the original lyrics of the Beatles' song 'Yesterday', the celebrated first edition of the works of Shakespeare, and Lenin's application for a British Library pass.

The British Library promises 'The knowledge of the world' and the Eduardo Paolozzi bronze in front of the new building represents Isaac Newton, whose discoveries revolutionized our perception of the world (below right). The four floors of the King's Library (left) contain a collection of 65,000 printed works once belonging to George III. The entrance gate (below left) was designed by Lida and David Kindersley.

ST PANCRAS INTERNATIONAL

St Pancras has been called the 'cathedral of the railways', a name that refers not only to its size and construction, but also to the Victorian lavishness of its decoration. The station was built in 1868 as a railway terminal connecting to the Midlands. At the time of its construction, the Barlow train shed, some 30 metres (100 feet) high and 73 metres (240 feet) wide, was the largest enclosed space in the world. After many years of dereliction the station has recently been completely restored and rebuilt. As St Pancras International it has been the terminus for the Eurostar since 2007, connecting London, Paris and Brussels via the Channel Tunnel. There are a further 15 platforms for regional trains, a bus station and a shopping mall with a selection of restaurants, pubs and cafés. The main red-brick Victorian hall is now a listed building.

The former Midlands Grand Hotel was used as office space by British Rail until 1985 (left). It has now been turned into luxury apartments and a five star Marriott Group hotel. The 9-metre (30-foot) high bronze under the station clock, by the British artist Paul Day, is called 'The Meeting Place' (below left). Below right: The magnificent restored and reglazed main hall, otherwise known as the Barlow Shed.

REGENT'S PARK

In 1818, the entire area of Regent's Park very nearly became a massive building site when the Prince Regent and future King George IV commissioned the architect John Nash to come up with a plan to develop this royal park. Nash designed a palace for his royal client, as well as handsome houses for the Prince Regent's friends, all to be surrounded by grand terraces that would complement the main buildings perfectly. The plan was only partially realized. Just eight of the proposed 56 houses were built, but the work did create the splendid-166 ha (410-acre) park we know today. It is the scene of all sorts of leisure activities, and home to some really noteworthy attractions. In its north-eastern corner, London Zoo is the oldest scientific zoo in the world. A canal marks the park's northern boundary, with Nash's elegant terraces lining its remaining sides.

The grey heron (below right) and other waterfowl have found a well-kept home in Regent's Park in the middle of London. Composed of lawns, flower beds, ponds and fountains, the whole area promises stressed Londoners a place for rest and relaxation. Couples and families can enjoy romantic hours in a rowing boat and the rose garden has 30,000 roses of 400 different species (left).

JOHN NASH

Success came late in life for architect John Nash (1752–1835), but in no uncertain terms, and this was to have consequences for elegant London. As a young man he trained as an architect but was not particularly successful; it is possible he lacked ambition, but he certainly had enough of a private income that he was not obliged to try too hard. Two circumstances changed this. He lost his fortune, and some of his smaller projects attracted the interest of the Prince Regent, who would later become George IV. The result was an ambitious project: whole districts were to be remodelled, the more imposing the better, and the royal palaces were also to be brought up to the most modern standards – a whim of a time when architecturally wonderful classical buildings, impossibly expensive even for London, were often to remain on the drawing board. Such royal patronage entailed successive commissions for new buildings and renovations throughout England, including the Royal Pavilion in Brighton, but Nash was unable to complete all his plans – or rather, his royal client ran out of money after his succession to the throne. Nonetheless, to this day Nash's architectural legacy includes some of the finest and most expensive buildings in the whole of London, whose elegance is timeless.

JOHN NASH

Cumberland Terrace (far left and below left) is one of John Nash's most famous works. The terrace consists of 31 houses, all of which remain in private hands. The entire row of 42 houses that make up Chester Terrace (below right) are listed buildings. A bust of John Nash can be found in All Souls Church at the north end of Regent Street, and this too was designed by the celebrated architect (left).

CAMDEN LOCK

From punks to hippies and goths, Camden Town is paradise for fans of any weird and wonderful cultural scene. Located just off the Regent's Canal, this small area, once home to Irish immigrants and until recently a hotspot of the Britpop scene, has become a really trendy part of town. Today, Camden Town's markets and music clubs make it a destination in its own right. In among the piles of tacky tourist merchandise you'll find alternative fashion (including lots of unique garments), crafts, bric-a-brac, and everything in between. When the market opened in 1974, it was no more than a few arts and crafts stalls. Today, the stalls stretch from Camden Lock right into the side streets, sharing the space with countless restaurants and food stands that together represent every ethnic cuisine. At weekends, the crowds get so big that passengers at the Underground station have to be directed by officials.

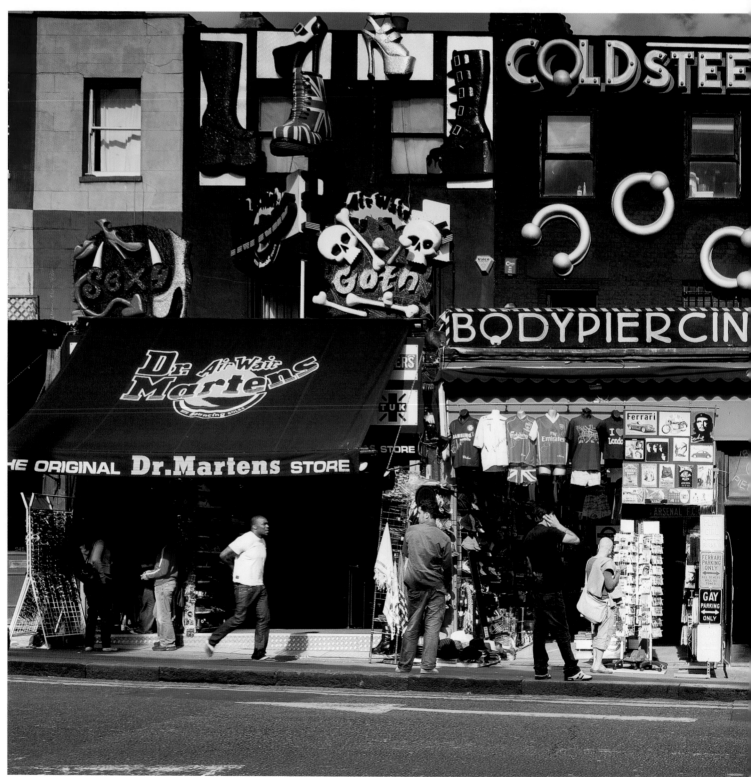

The area is named after Camden Lock, a manually operated lock on the local canal. The streets of Camden Town have stores catering to even the quirkiest tastes (below). The markets, both in the halls and passages and in the streets, are among the most popular in London and are real treasure troves of exotic street and youth culture items as well as vintage clothing (left).

HAMPSTEAD HEATH

Hampstead Heath is only 6 kilometres (less than 4 miles) from Trafalgar Square, but it is a world away from the bustle of the big city. With an area of 329 hectares (813 acres), London's oldest and largest park is no artificial construction, but a piece of unspoilt, if rather carefully tended, nature consisting of meadows, hills, woods (some of which are ancient), artificial lakes for bathing (some of which are reserved for men or women), playgrounds, sports fields, and even a few bits of remaining heath, to which the park owes its name. Enough of it has remained untouched to give the impression of being really out in the country. It even has its own police force, which maintains order by day and night. One of the most pleasant spots is the 98-metre (320-foot) high Parliament Hill at the south end of the heath, which enjoys an uninterrupted and entirely romantic view across London.

Elegant, 17th-century Kenwood House on the north edge of the heath (below) was left to the nation in 1927 by Lord Iveagh, a scion of the Guinness brewing family from Ireland, and has been open to the public ever since. Entitled 'The Writer', Giancarlo Neri's sculpture of a giant table and chair (left), exhibited on Hampstead Heath in 2005, is 9 metres (30 feet) high and intended to remind people of their creativity.

HIGHGATE CEMETERY

The cemetery's main claim to fame is the tomb of Karl Marx, who was buried here in 1883, but Highgate has many more celebrities, such as Douglas Adams ('The Hitchhiker's Guide to the Galaxy') and the sculptor Henry Moore, not to mention its unique location. The cemetery opened in 1839 and soon became a fashionable and sought-after last resting place (although no one was rushing to be buried there). The graves and mausoleums are a singular combination of Victorian extravagance, a fascination with death, kitsch and wealth, and the whole area resembles a set for a horror film, with unkempt bushes and trees, winding paths which always seem to lead to dark corners, lop-sided gravestones and mournful statues. To protect the site, viewing of the oldest and still by far the most beautiful part of the cemetery is only permitted as part of a guided tour.

'Workers of all lands, unite!' is engraved upon Karl Marx's tomb (below), although he is actually buried in the older part of the cemetery – the tomb was placed here to prevent too many workers gathering in the protected section of the cemetery. The gate to the Egyptian Alley (below left) is in the older section. The wild vegetation gives the cemetery an uncanny atmosphere (left).

SADLER'S WELLS

When Richard Sadler opened a 'Musick House' here in Islington in 1683, he quite literally found an additional source of income, with the discovery of a spring on his land which supposedly had healing properties. This initially attracted many of London's high society, but the spring lost its charms as quickly as the theatre; many other music houses sprang up closer to London, and even the healing spring was no longer a rarity. After numerous incarnations, the theatre finally found its niche with ballet. One of its most famous productions was Matthew Bourne's 1995 'Swan Lake', a contemporary interpretation in which all the swans were performed by men. Sadler's Wells, which has been located in its new premises since 1998, has become a reliable source of innovative contemporary dance as well as performances of classical ballet.

Sadler's Wells' new building (left) is not just a setting for modern interpretations of classical ballet and avant-garde dance performances; the totality of dance is embraced here, and there are many guest appearances. The Ballet Boys perform 'Naked' (below left); Butoh dancers from Sankai Juku in 'Kinkan Shonen' (below right, bottom); 'The Hard Nut' by the Mark Morris Dance Group (below right, top).

LONDON DERBIES

London derbies are not just football matches. They are tribal warfare with clear borders. Every London club has its own staked-out territory and supporters, and the strips and scarves in club colours are signs of this allegiance – at a glance, you know exactly who you are dealing with. Derby is a term meaning a local competition open to all, dating back to a time before football had established rules. The two halves of a village would play football against one another, and each team would defend the honour of its half of the village, differentiating itself proudly from the other half. This has changed little in the ensuing period. London has countless local football clubs, of which only five are in the Premiership. Arsenal ('the Gunners') and arch-rivals Tottenham Hotspur (known as Spurs for short) are the top clubs in North London, and games between them are known as North London derbies. The corresponding West London derby is between Chelsea, owned by the Russian oligarch, Roman Abramovitch, and Fulham, owned by Harrods boss Mohamed Al-Fayed. The fifth London Premiership club is West Ham United, who come from Upton Park in East London. A London derby is always a completely traditional experience, as indeed are the fights and skirmishes between the fans afterwards.

The clubs and their fans can be recognized by the colours they wear: Arsenal's colour is red with a cannon on their badge, and Tottenham Hotspur's is white, with a cockerel standing on a football. Chelsea players wear blue, with a lion holding a staff on the badge, and Fulham wears black and white with the letters FFC as their coat of arms. West Ham players wear claret and blue strips.

EAST LONDON

The East End has traditionally been one of London's most deprived areas. This part of the capital, east of the City and north of the Thames, is heavily developed. As the population expanded in the 19th century it became very overcrowded and the miserable living conditions here first gave rise to the term 'slum'. More recently an influx of young, middle-class residents has given the East End a whole new lease of life. On the Isle of Dogs, the new buildings of Canary Wharf have turned the area into London's second financial powerhouse, while Greenwich, an East End borough, is a World Heritage Site.

Now called Docklands, it was once the largest port area in the world and the pride of England's former sea power. After decades of dilapidation, the area was redeveloped with the prestige Canary Wharf project (in the background) which now dominates the skyline.

HACKNEY

Since the end of the 19th century, the East End has been a part of London often looked down upon by the 'finer' side of the city. The area was poor, a known den of criminality, and full of immigrants trying to find a foothold in the overpopulated suburbs east of the City. 'EastEnders' wasn't a popular television soap opera but more like a term of abuse. Things have changed, but even as the gentrification of East London continues apace, there is still some of the 'real' East End to be found in and around Hackney. In this densely populated and multicultural borough, Cockneys – a working-class group with a particular accent and unique slang – and immigrants from all over the world have established a unique community spirit, despite everything. The developments for the 2012 Olympic Games, a third of which are based in the borough, bring a new hope of prosperity to the area.

Only about half of Hackney residents identify themselves as 'white British'; the other half originally came from Asia, Africa and the Caribbean, as well as from other European countries. Each group has its own infrastructure, not only supporting its own community but also contributing to the characteristic blend that makes living in Hackney, or even visiting, such a singular experience.

BRICK LANE

The vibrant cultural mix of many parts of the East End is thanks to the people who settled here from former British colonies, including India, Pakistan and Bangladesh. Forced to find accommodation in the city's cheapest areas, they imbued them with their own culture and a touch of the exotic, enlivening London's drab streets. Locals call the area around Brick Lane, for example, Banglatown, in recognition of the area's large Bengali community.

Today, this lengthy thoroughfare is a curry lover's paradise, its row of balti, tandoori and curry restaurants interrupted only by a selection of sari stores, Asian grocery shops and import-export businesses. Brick Lane's Sunday market is a much-loved haunt for anyone hunting down unusual items, and if it's independent young designer fashion you're after, then this multicultural street will prove to be an equally rewarding treasure trove.

The Orient in the East End: there is an exotic bustle in Brick Lane, featured in Monica Ali's book of the same name, from art and graffiti to street music and the picturesque markets and colourful stores. East and West do not always co-exist as peacefully as the first glance might suggest. Cultural differences have sometimes led to tensions, and a mistrustful distance is maintained.

CANARY WHARF

For nearly 200 years, the Isle of Dogs – a section of land in a large meander of the River Thames – was London's busiest port. The area was not spared the destruction of World War II, and the docks – together with their rich heritage – were devastated in the bombing. But it was the introduction of containerization that was to be the final nail in the coffin of the docks. The end of the 20th century saw a dramatic rise in demand for modern office space and in 1988 – despite significant opposition – the construction of Canary Wharf on the run-down area of docklands commenced. The cluster of post-modern buildings provided a new home for both international banks and leading media organizations. Today, it is not only a symbol of a resurgent world business power, but also an image of London's future – a must-see for all enthusiasts of modern architecture.

Great Britain's three tallest skyscrapers: One Canada Square at 235 metres (771 feet), and the HSBC Tower and Citigroup Centre, both at 199 metres (653 feet), are at the heart of Canary Wharf (below). The architecture has more than a whiff of Manhattan about it and is among the most modern in Britain. The entrance to the underground station (left) looks like a giant spaceship.

ROYAL VICTORIA DOCK

The redevelopment of Docklands in London's East End involved not only the construction of prestigious office blocks but also the creation of whole new residential areas. The Royal Victoria Dock was once London's largest dock area, built in 1855 specially for large steamships and surrounded by enormous warehouses for the storage of meat, tobacco and fruit imported from the Americas. Nowadays, it is one of the finest examples of urban regeneration and includes prize-winning Britannia Village, a residential complex which contains the infrastructure of a complete village, ExCel London, a trade fair and conference centre where the London Boat Show takes place every year, and the spectacular Royal Victoria Dock Bridge, a 15-metre (50-foot) pedestrian bridge over the docks whose masts are intended to recall the tall ships of days gone by.

The architecture of the houses by the water in the Britannia Village complex is reminiscent of the original warehouses they replaced (below right). The impressive pedestrian bridge with its sailboat masts (below left) is accessed at both ends by lifts and stairs in the towers. During the annual London Boat Show, large yachts moor at the ExCel wharf (left) with its numerous cafés.

O2 DOME

This huge tent-like building is – when viewed from the air, at least – one of the city's most recognizable landmarks. Located on the Thames, the Millennium Dome was the third of the three Millennium projects with which London marked the beginning of the 21st century, along with the London Eye big wheel and the Millennium Bridge. When it first opened, the world's biggest dome turned out to be a bit of a flop. The exhibition of mankind that it hosted – exploring our identity, actions and habitat – closed after just one year, and nobody really knew quite what would become of the Dome until 2007, when a new name and role for the building was finally settled upon. The O2 (named after its sponsor, the mobile phone network) is now London's biggest entertainment complex, combining exhibition space with an 11-screen digital cinema and a multipurpose arena.

The O2 sits on the Greenwich peninsula riverside like a huge beached jellyfish, but it has a rich interior life. The building is an ideal concert venue as it is far enough away from residential areas that no one is disturbed. Pop music's greats have performed here, such as Madonna (left) on her 2009 Sticky & Sweet Tour. Important sports events (far left) are also part of the arena's schedule.

ROYAL NAVAL COLLEGE

The Old Royal Naval College, once the Royal Navy's training school, is the jewel in the crown of the Maritime Greenwich World Heritage Centre, an elegant complex of buildings on the south bank of the Thames, designed by Sir Christopher Wren, the architect of St Paul's Cathedral, and completed in 1712. The building was originally constructed as Greenwich Hospital to provide a home for wounded and retired Royal Navy personnel.

Lord Nelson, the most famous admiral of England's old fleet, lay in state here after his death in 1805. The hospital was closed in 1869 and served as a training school for naval officers until 1998. Nowadays it is under the care of the Greenwich Foundation trust, which maintains a visitors' centre, a gift shop, a café and a restaurant. Parts of the complex are also used by Greenwich University and the Trinity College of Music.

The most beautiful rooms in the complex are the Painted Hall (below left), the old baroque dining room with delightful paintings by James Thornhill, and the classical chapel (below right), which is often used for concerts because of its fine acoustics. The complex's river gates still bear the old Royal Hospital's coat of arms (left). The twin towers of the Naval College can be seen in the background.

GREENWICH

Justifiably praised for its harmonious beauty, since 1997 this famous area of south-east London has been a World Heritage Site entitled Maritime Greenwich. Along with the many historic houses in the borough, its scientific achievements, and the history of British sea power, the Old Royal Naval College and especially the Queen's House are part of the World Heritage Site. This little palace, designed by the illustrious architect Inigo Jones at the beginning of the 17th century (his first task following his appointment as surveyor to the king), was the first important classical building to be constructed in England. When the Naval College was built as the Naval Hospital in the 18th century, a royal decree determined that the view from the Queen's House was not to be interrupted, giving rise to the strange shape of the buildings that were to become the jewel in Greenwich's crown.

The hilly park behind the Queen's House has a view of the palace, the Naval College, and London, with the skyscrapers of Docklands in the background (previous pages). The Queen's House is now part of the National Maritime Museum and exhibits paintings with maritime themes. Its plain exterior conceals lavish interior decoration (below).

ROYAL OBSERVATORY

Greenwich may not be the centre of the world, but it is the centre of world time and the baseline for measuring longitude; the prime meridian, as established by British astronomers in 1851, runs straight through the middle of the observatory. Since 1885 it has been internationally recognized as the reference point for measuring time and determining longitude east and west of Greenwich. The Royal Observatory was the first building to be constructed in Great Britain exclusively for research purposes and was commissioned in 1675 by King Charles II, although not so much out of intellectual curiosity as to ease navigation using the stars and a seafarer's position relative to the motion of the earth. The building currently houses an exhibition of astronomical and navigational instruments as well as the most astounding and exact chronometers.

The time ball on top of Flamsteed House (left and below left) drops promptly at 1 pm GMT during winter (BST during summer), to set World Time. Nearby is the Shepherd Gate 24-hour clock, an early electric clock built in 1852. The prime meridian (below right), originally a brass strip, is now made of stainless steel. Since December 1999, a green laser beam has shone north over London at night to mark the meridian.

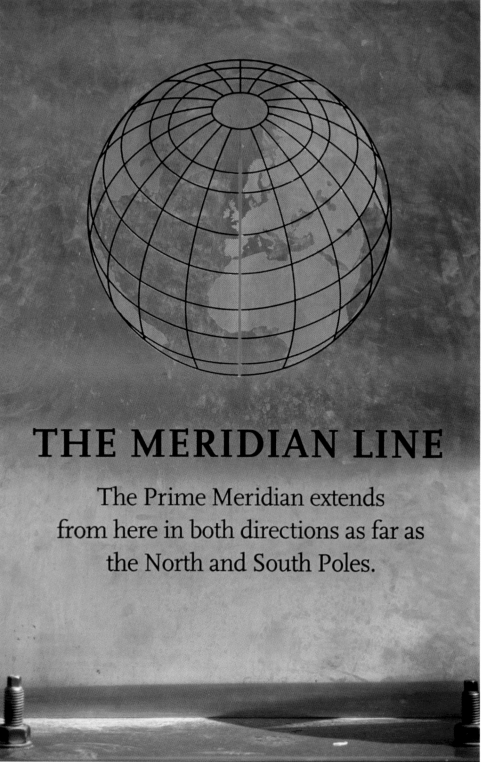

THE MERIDIAN LINE

The Prime Meridian extends from here in both directions as far as the North and South Poles.

THAMES BARRIER

London has always been in danger of flooding, caused either by heavy rain on the Thames flood plain that is unable to run off due to a high tide, or by North Sea storm surges and spring tides. The North Sea Flood of 1953, in which 300 people died in England alone, gave rise to the notion of constructing enormous flood defences at the mouth of the Thames. The problem was access for shipping to London Docks, for which sufficient room had to be left; however, this situation changed after freight shipping moved over to the use of containers and a new container port was constructed downstream at Tilbury. The new Thames Barrier, the world's second-largest sea defence after the Maeslantkering in the Netherlands, was built at Woolwich Reach between 1974 and 1982. If a storm surge is anticipated, the mighty gates can be closed in less than 90 minutes.

THAMES BARRIER

The ten rotating gates are usually lowered to the bed of the Thames, allowing river traffic to pass. When closed, the four main gates rise to a height of 20 metres (66 feet) above the water. The gates are raised once a month for test purposes, a fascinating sight which draws a crowd. Since their construction, there has been only one actual emergency, during the high tides of November 2007.

SOUTH BANK

The south bank of the Thames may only be a stone's throw from the City and London's other most desirable areas, but in the past it was rather disparaged by the capital's residents. Historically, this was the location of the city's main popular entertainment attractions and also its red-light district. Later, prisons and industrial facilities were built here, the latter running into crisis in the 20th century. More recently, the area has been helped by wide-ranging regeneration, shedding its old reputation to become instead a thriving hub of art and cultural life.

The Royal Festival Hall was built on the South Bank for the 1951 Festival of Britain and has attracted other cultural institutions to the site. Tate Modern (with its tall chimney) is a more recent addition, as is the half-timbered Globe Theatre, a reconstruction of the original.

THE DESIGN MUSEUM

Opening as the first of its kind in 1989, the Design Museum is small but perfectly formed. Although design now features in collections worldwide, the museum has retained its rank as one of the most prestigious; rather than retaining a permanent collection it presents regular special exhibitions of every aspect of design, including product and industrial design, architecture, furniture, graphic design and web publishing. The themes of the exhibitions are also diverse: some are conventional, such as a show featuring Manolo Blahnik shoes, while others are really innovative, such as one entitled 'Super Contemporary', held in 2009, which encouraged designers to present their weirdest plans for the London of the future. The likelihood of any of these visions ever coming to pass is remote, but they are a testament to the inventiveness of London designers.

The minimalist museum building was once a banana warehouse (left). The sculptor Eduardo Luigi Paolozzi's work in front of the museum is fittingly entitled 'Head of Invention' (below left). The 'inserts' in the head bear a quotation by Leonardo da Vinci about the creativity of Nature. Design usually focuses on products but can also be an end in itself, such as in this 2003 art installation (below right).

BUTLER'S WHARF

Butler's Wharf is a prime example of successful urban renewal, not just demolishing and rebuilding, but instead retaining some of the area's original historic character. These giant storehouses were constucted on the banks of the Thames in 1873 and were once London's largest warehouse complex, storing imported goods such as tea, coffee, cocoa, sugar and spices. After they were finally abandoned in 1972, a mixture of luxury apartments, offices, leisure facilities and restaurants was created, many of which belonged to the smart Conran chain. Apart from the Thames Path, which has a magnificent view of the Tower of London and Tower Bridge, the main attraction is Shad Thames, a narrow, cobbled street behind the warehouses still spanned by the old pedestrian bridges that used to link them – a veritable taste of Victorian London.

The old warehouses of Butler's Wharf have been lavishly restored and are not just to be found on the terraces along Shad Thames (left). The project includes further developments on Bankside to the west of Tower Bridge, where the Hays Galleria shopping and restaurant mall is located (below right). Pleasure boats and cruise ships sometimes moor here (below left). The wharf is now a Grade II listed building.

CITY HALL

Quite literally going off at a tangent: Greater London's City Hall houses the mayor's office and the 25 members of the London Assembly, and is yet another example of post-modern architecture in the British capital. The ten-storey building was constructed in 2002 and has already attracted several not altogether complimentary nicknames, including 'the onion' and 'Darth Vader's helmet', but the design was not just a whim of the architect, Norman Foster – it was carefully planned to offer optimal energy efficiency. The curved form of the building reduces the surface area, thus inhibiting heat loss, while the south-facing offices are stepped on the inside, providing natural shade and preventing overheating caused by the double glazing. The heat produced by computers and lighting is recycled and there are solar panels on the roof to collect energy.

There are numerous public spaces around City Hall, including an amphitheatre which is used for events in the summer, but the site itself has been leased for the London Assembly for only 25 years. A 500-metre (1,640-foot) long spiral inner walkway (below right) leads right to the top of the building, symbolizing transparency in government, and echoing Norman Foster's design for the Reichstag dome in Berlin.

LONDON'S BRIDGES

The Thames has always been London's lifeline. It supplied the city with water and food, connected it to the rest of Britain and the world, allowed trade to blossom, and thus ultimately laid the foundations for the growing power and wealth of a metropolis. Yet until the completion of Westminster Bridge in 1751, there was only one bridge across the river. That bridge was London Bridge, and its history dates back to the 1st century, when the Romans built the first wooden bridge across the river at that point. There have been several London Bridges over the centuries, and at times the shops along either side left only a narrow gap for traffic to pass. By 1733, crowding and congestion on London Bridge had become so bad that a decree was issued to all traffic to keep on the left-hand side of the road – possibly the reason that all British traffic now drives on the left. Today's London Bridge is a fairly unassuming structure that does at least accommodate several lanes of traffic. For centuries, however, it was left to ferries and small boats to connect the two sides of the river. As traffic increased, these were no longer sufficient, and the 19th century saw the construction of entirely new bridges. Further bridges were built more recently still, the Millennium Footbridge being the newest; there are now 34 bridges across the Thames in Greater London.

Albert Bridge (left) between Chelsea and Battersea is considered to be the prettiest bridge in London. It was opened to traffic in 1873 and has retained its Victorian decoration, although it is now reserved for light loads of no more than two tons. The Millennium Bridge (below), the most recent addition to London's bridges, connects Bankside and the City and is for the use of pedestrians only.

SOUTHWARK CATHEDRAL

Southwark Cathedral is just a few steps from London Bridge, and parts of its structure are among the oldest church buildings in London. The choir and its ambulatory, as well as the lower sections of the spire, date from the early 12th century. The choir, built around 1270, was an important feature of the former minster, while the high altar was added in the 15th century. The many tombs are a reminder of the church's early history, before it became the Anglican cathedral of the Diocese of Southwark in 1905. English poet and writer John Gower (14th C.) and Shakespeare's brother Edmund are both buried here. Shakespeare himself is commemorated by a monument erected in the south aisle in 1912. Near the cathedral, Borough Market is another enticing attraction, particularly for those interested in food. The market halls date from the mid-19th century, but the market itself is about as old as the church.

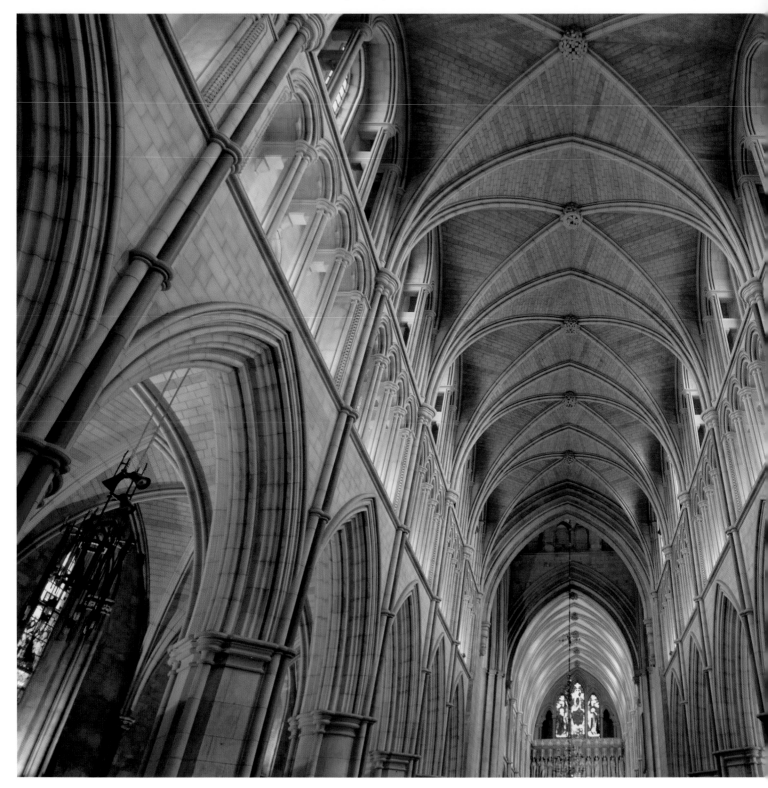

The breathtaking width and height of the nave draw the gaze to the impressive early-Gothic fan vaulting (below left and right). St George, seen here fighting the dragon (left), is the patron saint of England. The magnificent wall of carved figures in the choir (far left) includes saints, bishops and other individuals with a connection to the cathedral. Thomas Becket preached here just days before his murder in Canterbury.

SHAKESPEARE'S GLOBE THEATRE

It was in 1997 that Shakespeare's Globe finally reopened, just 200 metres (270 yards) from its original site. Its architecture, which is largely true to that of the original, and its productions, stripped of 'educated' interpretation, make a profound impression on its modern-day audience. The new Globe was constructed according to the original Elizabethan plans, so looks very much like it. The polygonal structure is almost circular, and the inner court is covered by the first and only thatched roof to have been laid in London since the Great Fire of 1666. Beneath it, there is a small covered stage and balcony, with three tiers of seating. It is standing room only in the pit, the central part of the auditorium, which is open to the elements. Ticket prices are consequently cheaper and the 'groundlings', as members of the audience in the pit are known, are permitted to come and go during the performance.

SHAKESPEARE'S GLOBE THEATRE

In Shakespeare's day, theatre was still broad entertainment for the masses rather than high art for the educated middle class, and this is how Shakespeare's plays, including classics such as 'Romeo and Juliet' (below right, bottom), are authentically and enthusiastically performed in the modern Globe. Shakespeare has featured in many films (below right, top), here in a 1977 television series about the master himself.

TATE MODERN

Situated on the south bank of the Thames, the Tate Modern building – with its 99-metre (325-foot) high tower – is an attraction in itself. Built after World War II, the building was originally a power station. Its transformation into a spectacular gallery of modern and contemporary art began in 1995, costing well over a hundred million pounds before it finally opened its doors in 2000. The turbine hall, which rises over five floors high, makes both an imposing entrance and a place to display commissions created specially for the space. Works by some of modern and contemporary art's most important artists are on show on the various gallery floors, including world-famous paintings by Picasso, Matisse, Mondrian and Dalí. There is also an incredible view over the Thames from the Tate's seventh-floor restaurant, looking out toward the City and St Paul's Cathedral on the opposite bank.

The exhibitions in Tate Modern change regularly, but the fascination of its industrial site is a constant. The Millennium Bridge connects the gallery to the historic City of London. One of the main attractions is the giant turbine hall (below left), for which a work of art is commissioned every year, such as the stainless-steel version of Louise Bourgeois' giant spider, 'Maman' (below right).

NATIONAL THEATRE / ROYAL FESTIVAL HALL

The South Bank is a massive dose of culture, stretching from Shakespeare's Globe Theatre in the east to County Hall in the west. Standing in the middle, the Royal Festival Hall was built for the 1951 Festival of Britain, an exhibition intended to celebrate new, post-war Britain. The Festival Hall, a venue for concerts and other events, has become the first post-war building to gain listed status. The Royal National Theatre (commonly known as the National Theatre, or simply 'the National') irresistibly draws the gaze to the other side of Waterloo Bridge. This Brutalist concrete building is the work of Denys Lasdun, although the severe formal requirements of the style are attenuated by his softer design. There are three stages in the complex, offering both classical and contemporary theatre as well as a residency for the Royal Shakespeare Company, among others.

Illumination at night reveals the many concrete layers of the National Theatre as a huge palace of culture (far left). Classical dramas such as Aeschylus' 'Oresteia' are performed along with Shakespeare's plays. Most of the concerts by the London Philharmonic Orchestra are held in the Royal Festival Hall (below left), which also stages occasional popular plays such as 'The Wizard of Oz' (below right).

THE HAYWARD GALLERY

The Hayward Gallery looks like a huge lump of concrete discarded on the banks of the Thames. Designed by a group of young architects and opened in 1968, its Brutalist concrete architecture was certainly not popular with every Londoner, but it has nonetheless become an essential part of the cultural complex at the core of the South Bank, along with the Royal Festival Hall and the Queen Elizabeth Hall. The gallery, which is dedicated to the visual arts, has no permanent collection but instead provides a space for large art exhibitions, which occasionally concentrate on one artist. In the past, shows have been devoted to such acknowledged masters as Leonardo da Vinci and Edvard Munch; however, in recent years the gallery has been concentrating more and more on contemporary art, for which the mighty concrete edifice provides a more appropriate setting.

An idyll in concrete: the art at the Hayward Gallery is not confined to the interior (left). The spaces available are ideal for Antony Gormley's giant sculptures, such as this piece, 'Space Station' (below left). The sculpture 'Staircase V', by the Korean artist Do Hu Suh, is large and yet delicate (below right, top). Ernesto Neto's sensuous installation 'Life fog frog...Fog frog' smells of spices (below right, bottom).

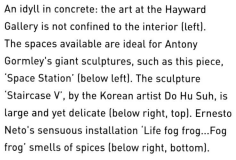

THE LONDON EYE

Opened amid great fanfare on New Year's Eve 1999, the 135-metre (443-foot) London Eye is the world's biggest big wheel. Located between County Hall and the Southbank Centre, it has become one of London's most popular tourist attractions. The wheel turns in a slow, continuous motion, taking about 30 minutes to complete a full rotation. Passengers can board one of the 32 capsules without the wheel having to stop. The fully glazed capsules afford visitors a commanding panoramic view over London and – in good weather – as far beyond the city as Windsor Castle. A basic ride on the wheel is fairly pricey, but for a wider outlay you can officially celebrate your birthday on board, or even get married. Though the London Eye was originally only intended to remain on the river for five years, it has proved such a success that it is now due to stay in place for some time to come.

The view from the top of the London Eye is dizzying, not just because of the great height of the wheel but also because the vast extent of the city becomes apparent. In good weather you get a clear view of more than 50 of the main sights. The London Eye has been compared to the Eiffel Tower in Paris or the Empire State Building in New York as a fitting symbol for a metropolis.

WATERLOO STATION

With more than 20 platforms and a surface area of some 100,000 square metres (over a million square feet), Waterloo is the largest railway station in Great Britain, and it took on another record in 2009: the main platforms were fitted with the longest row of automatic gates in the country. There is even a number of shops supplying refreshments and every other need for passengers visiting the station, and yet its beginnings were far more modest. The station opened in 1848, but rising demand meant that it had to be extended and modernized at the turn of the 20th century. Rechristened Waterloo International between 1994 and November 2007 as the London terminus of Eurostar, it has now had to cede the title as St Pancras has taken over that role. Nowadays Waterloo is the terminal for all trains coming from south-west England.

Victory Arch, the station's main entrance (exit 5), is a memorial to fallen railway workers in both world wars (left). The figures beneath the statue of Britannia represent War and Peace. The five Eurostar platforms are currently unused, as rebuilding them for local traffic is proving to be too expensive at the moment. There are 19 other busy platforms and another four in Waterloo East station next door.

STREET ART

Decried as vandalism by many, graffiti is an art form carried out by young people under the cover of darkness, using spray cans of paint to leave tags, pictures, and witty, political, or simply meaningless comments, which are rapidly removed by the authorities. Until the arrival of Banksy, that is. Banksy created images and drawings that were not only subversive but also astonishing, because of both their bold locations and their critical and yet undeniably humorous statements. First the media took an interest, then the art scene, and soon Banksy had become a sensation, even though his work was still officially illegal. As a result, once-reviled graffiti now goes under the description of 'urban art' and regularly attracts five-figure sums on the art market. Banksy has become an established figure, although his identity is still a secret, and he has of course found imitators, with street artists such as Adam Neate, D*face, Pure Evil, and Eine leaving their own equally witty and artistically accomplished works in streets across London. The area around Shoreditch and Spitalfields in East London in particular has become a kind of open air gallery. Banksy's work has even been celebrated in a major exhibition in the museum in Bristol, his home town, proving that graffiti can indeed be art.

Street art is ephemeral and sometimes lasts for only a few days; much graffiti survives only as a photograph. Banksy's works have become famous, although not necessarily in their original locations (below left). Below right: Pieces created by master graffiti artists during the 2008 Cans Festival held in a tunnel under Waterloo Station. Left: Street art in Brick Lane in the East End.

FURTHER AFIELD

Beyond London lies a network of castles, houses and estates, from grand palaces to modest mansions. Not all these splendid buildings are open to the public – the British nobility is, after all, still very much in residence, but the royal palaces are at least partly accessible to visitors. Hampton Court has been little occupied by British monarchs since the latter half of the 18th century, but Windsor Castle has been inhabited by royalty since the Middle Ages. The Queen decided to make the castle her main weekend home when she came to the throne in 1952; it is often also now used for state banquets.

Windsor Castle, the largest still-inhabited royal castle in the world (below), is often described as the Queen's weekend place; she prefers to rest from her official duties there, even though it is occasionally used to receive state guests.

KEW GARDENS

Botanical gardens always draw a crowd, but Kew Gardens, the official Royal Botanic Gardens located in Kew, is a garden of superlatives and a World Heritage Site into the bargain. It has grown from a small 3.6-hectare (9-acre) site in the 18th century to today's complex of 102 hectares (252 acres) with the largest plant collection in the world. At its heart are the two largest Victorian hothouses, the Palm House and the Temperate House for vegetation from moderate climates. These two world-famous wrought-iron and glass buildings are surrounded by other smaller hot-houses, decorative buildings and museums. Other attractions include the Bonsai House, the Waterlily House (with the hottest climate in the gardens) and the Evolution House, an exciting recapitulation of 3,500 millions years of plant development (look out for the dinosaur footprints).

The glass panes in the Palm House are all hand-blown, and the climate is the same as that of a tropical rainforest (below). The vegetation, which includes spices, fruits and plants with medicinal and other uses, is divided by its geographical distribution, apart from the area under the dome, where the tallest palms grow. In the winter of 2007/8, the garden was decorated with giant sculptures by Henry Moore (left).

SYON HOUSE / SYON PARK

Syon House is one of England's most elegant country houses and has been owned by the same dynasty for more than 400 years – the Dukes of Northumberland. The estate is named after the abbey that formerly occupied the site, which in turn derived its name from Mount Zion. The abbey was dissolved by Henry VIII in the 16th century and the house was built shortly afterwards by the Duke of Somerset, finally being acquired by Henry Percy, the 9th Earl of Northumberland. In the 18th century, the first Duke of Northumberland had several rooms redesigned by the renowned Scottish architect Robert Adam and they have retained their neoclassical magnificence. The grounds were landscaped by Lancelot 'Capability' Brown in the then new English style, and countless rare trees and plants now grow in the magical gardens, which are listed in their own right.

The large hothouse built in 1826 is a little palace of stone, glass and metal, and was originally intended as a setting for the exotic plants collected by the duke of the time (below). The pastel tones and black-and-white marble floor of the Great Hall (far left) exude under-stated elegance, whereas the Ante Room (left) is furnished with colourful marble and gilt statues of various gods.

RUGBY

Rugby is a rougher variant of football, especially when it comes to the often hazardous 'scrum', but the sport is nonetheless more popular in middle-class circles. This is perhaps due either to its origins or to its still relatively exclusive appeal. The ball game was 'invented' in the 19th century at Rugby School in the little town of Rugby in Warwickshire. English public schools were intended to produce gentlemen to serve the Empire, and Rugby, one of the oldest in England, is still a leading school with many famous alumni, including the former prime minister Neville Chamberlain and the writer Salman Rushdie. However, the school's most famous pupil is perhaps one William Webb Ellis, who attended Rugby when it was still the original grammar school, founded in 1567. In 1823 this accidental hero, faced with defeat in a house football match, is said to have picked up the ball in his hands and run with it, before placing it in the opposing goal. Thus the game of rugby was formed. At the time football had no hard and fast regulations, and when these were eventually laid down a faction separated off and formed the Rugby Football Union. The first Rugby World Cup was held in 1897 and is now played every four years. The trophy is named the Webb Ellis Cup after the game's inventor.

Several rugby tournaments take place world-wide, including the popular Six Nations held between the European teams of England, Ireland, Wales, Scotland, France and Italy. A side consists of 15 players, including eight hearty forwards and seven speedy backs. Rugby was an amateur sport until 1995 and the game and the players have only become professional since then.

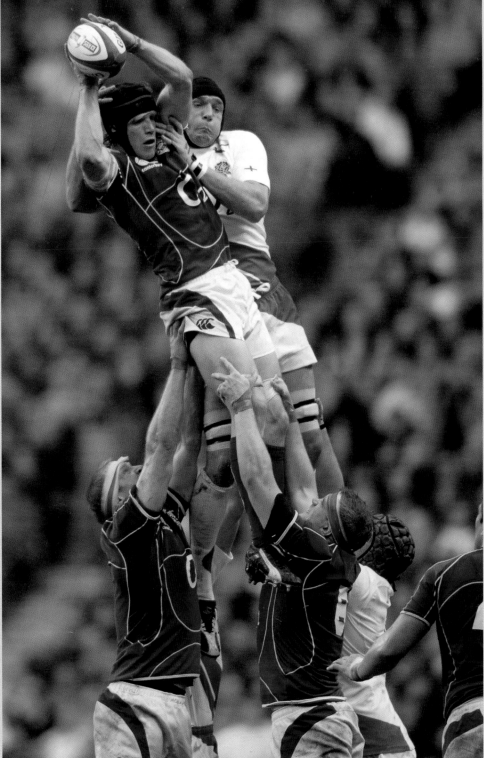

HEATHROW AIRPORT

Landing at Heathrow Airport gives you the best bird's-eye view of London – an endless sea of urban sprawl stretching to the horizon. Heathrow is the hub of European air travel and one of the largest airports in the world; its annual turnover of 67 million passengers is certainly the largest. Its less than perfect location, which entails an approach from the east over the city, is due to its origins as a test airfield; it was given over to civil aviation only in 1946. This once tiny aerodrome now covers a total area of 12.4 square kilometres (nearly 5 square miles) and has five terminals and several hotels, as well as other facilities. The airport's Terminal 5 was opened in 2008 for long-distance flights and is the largest free-standing building in Great Britain. A controversial sixth terminal and a third runway are planned for within the next ten years.

Heathrow's new Terminal 5 (left) is intended to handle as many as 35 million passengers a year and is reserved for long-distance flights and British Airways, the UK flag carrier, for whom Heathrow is the home airport. More than 90 airlines fly to Heathrow, serving 170 destinations. As the airport is only 25 metres (80 feet) above sea level, it is particularly susceptible to fog.

WINDSOR CASTLE

When the royal family needed a new name, it was to Windsor Castle that they turned for inspiration. Britain's oldest castle, it has also been occupied without interruption for the longest period. It has stood on this spot, to the west of London, for nearly a thousand years. Originally built as a fortress by William the Conqueror around 1070, Windsor has been extended, altered and inhabited by a succession of kings, who variously used it as a fortress, prison and garrison. Most of the structure we see today dates from the 14th century, when Edward III added the State Apartments, Round Tower and Norman Gateway. The last major restructuring took place at the beginning of the 19th century, under George IV. Along with Holyrood in Edinburgh and Buckingham Palace in London, Windsor Castle is one of the three official royal residences, and is the Queen's favourite weekend retreat.

Windsor Castle has a traditional changing of the guard with a military band (left), just like at Buckingham Palace. Furnished in regal splendour, the rooms in the castle, such as the Green Room (below left), the Queen's ballroom (below right, top), which is hung with paintings of 19th-century princes and princesses, and the Waterloo Chamber (below right, bottom), are used for state occasions.

ST GEORGE'S CHAPEL

St George's Chapel, part of the imposing Windsor Castle, is a late English Gothic masterpiece and its size and magnificence resemble those of a cathedral rather than a chapel. Its splendour was preserved during the Reformation as the chapel was under the direct protection of the monarch and the College of St George, which is devoted to England's patron saint. It is also the mother church of the Order of the Garter, one of Great Britain's most exclusive chivalric orders, which consists of the current sovereign, the heir to the throne and 24 other knights. The order was founded in the 14th century and is intended to recall the knights of King Arthur's round table. Numerous kings and their families have been buried in the chapel, from Edward IV (1493) and Henry VIII (1547) to the Queen Mother (2002), the much-loved mother of Elizabeth II.

The heraldic banners belonging to the members of the Order of the Garter hang over the choir stalls, where each member has a seat for life (below left). The knights assemble every year in June in the chapel and castle. The altar, beneath which Edward IV, among others, is buried, is skilfully carved and topped with an enormous stained-glass window (below right). Left: A stunning detail of the ceiling of the nave.

ASCOT

The annual Royal Ascot race meeting takes place in a small town south of Windsor in the middle of June and has been the highlight of the horse-racing season since Queen Anne founded the race course here in 1711. The Queen arrives in a splendid coach every day during the four-day event, accompanied by members of her family, and the races rather pale in comparison. Ascot is a social event of the first importance where the English upper classes meet and mingle, although the meeting has had to remain open to the public since a parliamentary decree of 1813. More than 300,000 people visit the races every year, often not because of any interest in horses at all, but instead born of a desire to attend a spectacle at which the royal family as well as many members of the British upper classes will be present in all their perhaps sometimes excessive finery.

To get into the Royal Enclosure, the VIP area around the royal family, you need not only good connections – guests may only attend at the invitation of an established member – but also the correct outfits: morning suit and top hat for gentlemen, and ladies must cover their shoulders and heads (left), which sometimes leads to rather fanciful trends in headgear, especially on Ladies' Day.

MARBLE HILL HOUSE / HAM HOUSE

The area by the Thames between Richmond and Hampton Court is not exactly the Loire Valley, but the river here has always been lined with many little castles and country houses, belonging either to the minor nobility or to the king's mistresses. One of the oldest is Ham House, a house unique in Europe, as it is the only more or less perfectly preserved authentic 17th-century country seat. It was built in 1610 by Sir Thomas Vavasour but the interior decoration, which can still be admired to this day, was not carried out until the late 17th century, under the command of the Duchess of Lauderdale. Marble Hill House, on the other hand, is a purely Palladian, early 18th-century villa, constructed for Henrietta Howard, the mistress of George II. It is the last complete villa to survive from the period and is stylishly furnished with original fittings.

Ham House's grounds (below) are just as original as the house, which is reputed to be the most haunted in England: it is said to be frequented by the ghosts of the Duchess of Lauderdale and her dog. Henrietta Howard, the chatelaine of Marble Hill House (left), was a highly educated woman and many intellectual visitors attended her salon, including the writer Jonathan Swift.

RICHMOND PARK

With an area of about 1,000 hectares (4 square miles), Richmond Park is the largest of London's royal parks and also the largest enclosed municipal park in Europe. The wall was built by Charles I in 1637 to enclose his hunting grounds and was not appreciated by his new neighbours; Charles had relocated his entire court to Richmond Palace the same year to escape the plague that was raging through London. The palace was demolished less than 20 years later, but the park and the wall survived. There are several pedestrian entrances and even a couple for vehicles, which are bound by a speed limit of 30 km/h (20 mph) and only allowed in during the day. No music may be played in the park and barbecues are banned, making it an oasis of peace. It is also a nature reserve, affording a wide variety of animal and plant life an undisturbed place to live and grow.

Richmond Park is famed for its abundant game. Some 650 red and fallow deer live here in the wild (below), although their numbers are reduced in an annual cull that takes place in November. The park consists of meadows, small woods and copses (left), crossed by footpaths, bridleways and cycle tracks. There are several historic buildings and gardens scattered throughout the park.

WIMBLEDON

The private All England Croquet and Lawn Tennis Club first held a men's singles competition in the London suburb of Wimbledon in 1877, making the Wimbledon Championships the oldest tennis tournament in the world. It is also considered the most prestigious of the four Grand Slam competitions, the most important international tennis tournaments, and is the only one of the four still to be played on grass. The current stadium and its surrounding courts were built on this site in 1922 and has witnessed matches by tennis legends such as Björn Borg, Boris Becker, Steffi Graf, Martina Navratilova, Pete Sampras and many others who will be known to anyone who has even a passing interest in tennis. Wimbledon fortnight is still a big media event of international interest and parliamentary legislation is in place to ensure the finals are broadcast on terrestrial television.

Inaugurated in 2009, a moveable roof on the Centre Court now protects matches from the rain. The traditional Wimbledon colours are purple and dark green, although nowadays umpires and ball boys and girls wear a dark blue uniform (left); players must wear white. Below: The gilt cup is awarded to the men's singles champion; the winner of the ladies' singles receives a silver plate.

HAMPTON COURT

Like so many English palaces, Hampton Court was not originally built as a royal residence, but was instead later taken over by the crown. Over the centuries, various monarchs commissioned splendid extension and restructuring schemes to create what is now considered one of the most beautiful historic palaces in the London area. Cardinal Wolsey, Henry VIII's Lord Chancellor, acquired the 14th-century estate in 1514 and set about trans-

forming it into a great Renaissance palace. When Wolsey later fell from grace, Henry VIII took Hampton Court for himself and extended and redesigned it in the Tudor style. Later, new wings were added, designed by Sir Christopher Wren. Among the palace's attractions are the Great Hall, dating from 1532, the astronomical clock at the Anne Boleyn Gatehouse, the huge kitchens and the Royal Tennis Court – not to mention the odd ghost or two.

William III commissioned Christopher Wren to redesign the garden wing of Hampton Court in the 17th century. The formal garden dates back to the same period but has had more flower beds added in recent years. The palace is mostly work commissioned by Henry VIII (left). Far left: 'An Allegory of Tudor Succession', a painting from 1572 on display at Sudeley Castle in Gloucestershire.

INDEX

PICTURE CREDITS

MONACO BOOKS is an imprint of Verlag Wolfgang Kunth
© Verlag Wolfgang Kunth GmbH & Co.KG, Munich, 2009

Text: Petra Dubilski
English translation: JMS Books LLP (translation: Michael Gray, Malcolm Garrard; editior: Jenni Davis; design: cbdesign)

For distribution please contact:
Monaco Books
c/o Verlag Wolfgang Kunth, Königinstr. 11
80539 München, Germany
Tel: +49.89.45 80 20 23
Fax: +49.89.45 80 20-21
info@kunth-verlag.de
www.monacobooks.com
www.kunth-verlag.de

Printed in Slovakia

ISBN 978-389944-538-1